Five minutes to midnight

James Stewart

Five minutes to midnight

James Stewart and mission to Europe

T. Omri Jenkins

EVANGELICAL PRESS

EVANGELICAL PRESS
12 Wooler Street, Darlington, Co. Durham, DL1 1RQ, England

British Library Cataloguing in Publication Data available

ISBN 0 85234 266 7

Unless otherwise indicated, Scripture quotations in this publication are from the Authorized (King James) version, or (in the foreword) the New King James Version.

Cover picture reproduced by courtesy of Dave Pepler.
Plates on the following pages are reproduced by courtesy of the following:

Page 62	Paul Ottavio
Page 116	Doris Simmonds
Pages 92, 109	Derek Smith
Pages 41, 57	Betty Stevens

Printed in Great Britain by Courier International, Tiptree, Essex.

To the memory of

James Stewart

and to

Dorothy,

my dear wife,

without whose love and loyal support

there would have been nothing for me to write.

Contents

Preface

The writing of this book was begun several years ago but has repeatedly had to give way to other, more pressing demands, many of which show few signs of abating.

It is my hope and prayer that, in God's mercy, this account will stimulate all who read it to work and pray for modern Europe and for all who faithfully preach the unadulterated gospel in the various countries of that continent. Most of all, I pray that the Lord of the harvest, who gave revival to James Stewart in several of those countries, will once again come upon his people in like manner.

Heartfelt thanks are due to many friends for help in preparing and producing this book, especially to my former secretary Doris Simmonds, who has typed and retyped my scribblings with her customary patience and accuracy. Above all, thanks be to God for the privilege of serving him in and for Europe.

T. Omri Jenkins
August 1989

Foreword

'A man of Macedonia stood and pleaded with [Paul], saying, "Come over to Macedonia and help us." Now after he had seen the vision, immediately we sought to go to Macedonia, concluding that the Lord had called us to preach the gospel to them.'

This was a clear call to the first missionaries to take the gospel to Europe. It was in strange contrast to their previous experience, when 'they were forbidden by the Holy Spirit to preach the word in Asia. After they had come to Mysia, they tried to go into Bithynia, but the Spirit did not permit them.' It was evidently the Spirit's purpose that Paul should travel at this precise time with the gospel, not into Asia, but to Europe.

In this book, we read of the still beckoning European appealing, 'Come over and help us.' Imagine in Paul's day the seeming incongruity of such a plea. Greece was the seat of the world's greatest philosophers, the cradle of democracy, a centre of art and culture. Philippi, to which Paul was directed, was a leading city of Macedonia, a replica in miniature of Rome, the great metropolis of the known world; where law, organization and engineering had reached a pinnacle. The Macedonians knew the best of both worlds, Greece and Rome, yet it was *their* need that evoked the beseeching call: 'Help us!'

It was a privilege and a joy to meet James Stewart and his family in 1955, and especially to hear him preach. It is refreshing now to be reminded of the remarkable way in which he was used of God during the pre-war years in European countries, many of which are now incorporated into the Soviet Zone. For those of us who have a yearning to see the hand of God moving again in an unmistakable spiritual awakening, it is encouraging to know that the present work in Europe had its origin in 'revival fires'.

It is apparent that the need for an organized missionary fellowship arose out of the spiritual fruitfulness that attended James Stewart's ministry. Doubtless he had no idea that this work would be so richly and continually blessed. There was nothing contrived about the inception of the European Evangelistic Crusade, as it became known; it was a consequence of remarkable indications that this was 'a field white already to harvest'.

My long-time friend and colleague Omri Jenkins has not disguised the limitations, nor the trauma associated with the development of the work. He has painted the picture 'warts and all'. We have here an honest account, a clear understanding of the gracious way in which the Lord has ordered his work so that 'the things that have happened have fallen out rather to the furtherance of the gospel'. With characteristic understatement he refers to himself as 'the present writer', who followed in the leadership of the work in succession to the Rev. Donald Stuart. As one connected with the work from then on, and able to observe the changing pattern, I can say that, on the human level, the European Missionary Fellowship, as it is now known, owes Omri Jenkins an incalculable debt, not only for his vision, dynamism, organizational and pastoral gifts, but also for his clear grasp of the biblical principles which should underlie and govern all missionary endeavour.

These principles include the following:

- to evangelize with the purpose of church planting;
- to train and equip national Christians to become the pastors, leaders and evangelists in their own churches;
- to seek as God enables, to establish local, indigenous, self-supporting, evangelizing churches;
- to send out those called by God from among us in the closest co-operation with their home churches;
- to have on the executive committee of the fellowship leaders and ministers who accept responsibility for pastoral care and who visit specific areas to

encourage and to minister to those who work in pioneer situations.

These are some of the hallmarks which have been impressed on the EMF by a wise and statesmanlike leadership.

Many parts of this book I found particularly informative and salutary. There are valuable insights into the actual situation in Europe. The brief but careful references to political and social history, including pre- and post-Reformation influences, help to make it a valuable source of information for any reader who has a concern for the needs of these days. We have an analysis of the opportunities for the gospel, and also of the adversaries of the gospel. We have a solemn picture of secularized Europe, more destitute of authentic Christian witness than continents such as Africa or South America. Countries that once were the source of missionaries are now themselves in great need of having the gospel preached in them.

The challenge is surely apparent when we see, on the one hand, a creeping secularization, and on the other, the efforts being made to create a uniform 'Christian religion', claiming to represent and speak for all except the 'eccentric' minority, not considered worthy of recognition, who may be denied opportunities for the expression of revealed truth. The march of Islam could mean that by the year 2025 considerable sections of Europe will be numerically and politically dominated by an anti-Christian religion.

These are factors which should make us question how seriously we take the Lord's command to pray the Lord of the harvest that he might thrust forth labourers into his harvest field. More labourers with vision and Holy Spirit direction, with obedience and commitment, are needed today, as in our Lord's day, in Paul's day, and in the days of those like James Stewart who have followed in his steps. There is now an opportunity for us to obey; it may not always be so. We can now support, with more commitment, in prayer and in practical ways, those who are still able to go and work in the harvest field.

Pray God that there will be a response to this urgency, and that we may yet see a new day of endeavour to take the gospel to every creature before it is too late; a new day of the Son of Man when he rides forth on the white horse of gospel purity, conquering and to conquer, throughout this our beloved needy continent.

Paul Tucker

1.
'Glory to God! Glory to God!'

Late in the year 1934 a young man arrived in Riga, which was then the capital city of the small but independent Baltic republic of Latvia. Fatigued by the long third-class journey in draughty and densely-packed trains, he found that the severe cold of the Baltic winter was more than his inadequate British clothing could withstand. Emerging from the station at four in the morning, he felt faint from hunger and weariness and fell, but, clutching a lamp-post, he pulled himself up and began to pray with some desperation. He had come to Riga believing that God had called him to preach the gospel in eastern Europe, and he now cried to God for help. Suddenly, he remembered a piece of paper a Christian lady in Scotland had pushed into his hand before he left. 'When you are lonely and discouraged,' she had said, 'read these verses.' The paper was in his pocket Bible and he now looked up its references:

Exodus 33:14: 'My presence shall go with thee, and I will give thee rest.'

Judges 6:14: 'Go in this thy might… have not I sent thee?'

Mark 16:20: 'And they went forth and preached everywhere, the Lord working with them, and confirming the word with signs following.'

Reassured through the Scriptures and prayer, he went into the strange city confident that the Lord would undertake for him.

James Alexander Stewart was just twenty-four years of age when he travelled from Glasgow to Riga. He knew only the English language, which he spoke with a strong Scots accent, and the one vague contact he had was the name of William Fetler, who was then the leader of the Salvation Temple in the city. Fetler had trained at Spurgeon's College in London and had been dubbed the 'Spurgeon of Latvia'. James had read about him in Christian magazines and knew that he had a thriving evangelistic work in Riga, but he did not know Fetler's address.

It was to William Fetler's brother Robert that the young Scot's steps were directed after repeated garbled enquiries. Robert Fetler was the pastor of a Baptist church in the city, and a few short years later when Russia overran the little Baltic countries, he would be banished to Siberia, where he died. But now in Riga he took the stranger in and provided him with a much-needed bed where he slept the clock round. Robert viewed James as sent by God in answer to much prayer, but brother William was more sceptical, finding it difficult to accept an unknown and uninvited man who knew no word of Latvian or Russian, yet who still claimed the Lord had brought him to Riga to evangelize. It transpired that prayer meetings for revival were being held at the Temple that very week, and James Stewart was allowed five minutes during one of these to give a short testimony. The pastor who translated was satisfied by what he heard and allowed the visitor ten minutes at the next meeting. This was followed by thirty minutes, and then the main ministry in the subsequent evening meetings was entrusted to Stewart.

The week's meetings ended, William Fetler suggested an immediate evangelistic mission with James Stewart as the evangelist, but arrangements had already been made with Robert for a mission in his Baptist church, where pastor and people had been praying earnestly for revival. Their cries had been heard and they were to be answered abundantly in the meetings which now began. James Stewart recorded later that 'The heavens were opened and the floods descended.' 1200 people packed the building each night and amazing scenes followed. Many meetings finished in the early hours of the morning and more than once when the preacher had left the building after the evening service, he had to return and begin again at around midnight, with the building still full to capacity.

This first mission in the Baptist church ended, another one began in the Salvation Temple and here, said Stewart, 'Mighty movements of the Spirit were witnessed.' William Fetler was himself a remarkable man of whom the great Spurgeon's son Thomas said, 'If my father's seminary had done nothing else than to produce dear Pastor William, it was still worthy of its existence.' William had visited Wales during the 1904/5 revival, had met Evan Roberts and had seen for himself great evidence of the power of the Spirit at work in the Principality. He was never the same afterwards, his great burden being that God would send revival to Latvia and Russia. His prayer was heard, and revival came through the meetings which now began and which were to continue for five months, with over 2,000 people attending every day. But, said James Stewart later, it was not only the size of the crowds that gathered: 'It was the awful sense of the majesty and holiness of God: it was the liberty of the Spirit.' The meetings sometimes went on round the clock, with as many people present at two in the morning as in the afternoon! 'Nobody knew how long a service would last; nobody bothered about the clock; nobody wanted to leave.'

The strenuous demands of the revival in Riga took their toll on James Stewart and he was advised to seek rest for his body and mind. With this in view he went to the neighbouring republic of Estonia. But the rest and relaxation he sought evaded him as he saw the multitudes as 'sheep without a shepherd'. He began to pray and it was not long before he contacted a Baptist pastor in Tallinn, the capital city, who was also praying for revival. This pastor immediately visited as many as possible of his flock, informing them that meetings would begin the next day, a Friday, and that the speaker would be a Scotsman. God's time had come for them too, and by Sunday the building was overcrowded, and soon it became too small even for the morning meetings for prayer and Bible teaching. Evening meetings were moved to a large Lutheran church but this too proved inadequate. Christians were asked to stay at home and to pray so that unbelievers could be accommodated, but still there was not enough room. A large public hall seating several thousands was secured, but even this proved too small though three or four meetings were held every day.

Arriving at the hall one evening, James found a crowd outside the doors and was told the place was full. By now he was weary in body and mind and he wondered how he could face the multitude that night. He made his way to the basement, intending to cry to the Lord for renewed strength, but on entering the dark room he heard voices. Finding the switch, he turned on the light and saw a group of women on their faces before God, pleading that he would bless the meeting upstairs. The sight immediately revived the preacher in body and soul. Switching out the light, he went back upstairs to face the throng, assured that God would do his own work.

Eventually James Stewart lost his voice in Tallinn and to regain it he went to a seaside town near the Soviet border. This place had no Protestant church and, once his voice was restored, he was soon trying to arrange meetings. The need for a translator was paramount and he found one in a lady who taught English at the local university. She was not a Christian; indeed she freely admitted that she had never had a Bible in her hand and knew nothing of the things of God. Stewart had not used a lady translator before, still less an unbelieving one, and he had grave doubts about proceeding. However, he remembered how David Brainerd had preached to the American Indians through a translator who was the worse for wear with drink, and how much blessing had followed. Feeling somewhat reassured, he went ahead, believing that God could do in Estonia what he had done in the American forests. The meetings were announced as 'Lectures on the Bible' and the people were invited to bring pencils and notebooks with them. A supply of New Testaments was secured and a copy was handed to each person who came. Scenes similar to those witnessed in Riga and Tallinn were soon repeated and many souls were converted, not least the interpreter, who rejoiced with others in Christ and his salvation.

On the last evening the interpreter asked James to go with her to visit an elderly man. She had already witnessed to this man and he was waiting for such a visit. Following the meeting and its aftermath, the preacher and the professor finally reached their aged friend around midnight. As the plan of salvation was expounded to him using appropriate verses (Isaiah 53:6: Romans 3:23, John 3:16) the man suddenly rose to his feet, and with gospel light shining within, began to praise God, exclaiming, 'Glory to God! Glory to God!' as he walked around the room. He suddenly stopped and asked, 'How many people know about this verse?' (John 3:16). 'Oh, millions in my country and America,' came the reply. 'Then why have you not told me this before I became an old man?' he asked. There was no satisfactory answer to give to that.

The man's spontaneous question, with its profound

implications, put into words the conviction which God had used to bring James Stewart to that Baltic scene. This is what had moved him from his early conversion and continued to motivate him to the end of his days. He was soon on his way to other countries of eastern Europe and the revival blessing experienced in Latvia and Estonia would be repeated in varying degrees in one country after another, up to the outbreak of World War II and the months that followed. It was from these remarkable visitations that the European Missionary Fellowship was to emerge in due time.

2.
Glasgow's boy preacher

James Stewart was born and brought up in Glasgow. Both his parents were from Northern Ireland, although it was in Glasgow that they met each other and were married. They were godly believers who ordered their humble home and raised their family of six children in accordance with the Word of God. James was the second of five boys, with one sister, who was the eldest child. Their father, who had been orphaned at an early age in Lurgan near Belfast, suffered from poor health and was taken from this life when James was only fourteen. The burden of the home thus fell upon Mrs Stewart, but despite many privations, the gospel had pride of place, with the family altar in daily practice. James used to say in later years that in his young days, 'We had salvation on both sides of the fireplace!' and, 'Mother sang us to sleep at night with the hymns of Zion.' The cause of missions too always had a high priority in family prayer and in the meagre finances of the home.

With an ailing father, and in days when the Welfare State was still a political pipe-dream, from an early age the children had to augment the family income by undertaking various simple jobs. James' first job was on a farm on the outskirts of Glasgow, where he had to drive the cows from the fields for milking and back again, both morning and evening. He was just six when this responsibility was first entrusted to him and it meant rising before six on dark mornings to collect the cows from pastures up to two miles distant from his home. Other jobs followed - delivering newspapers, milk and the freshly-baked bread rolls so favoured in many parts of Scotland. He still had enough time, however, to play football, and as his skill developed he became one of the football-mad youngsters of Glasgow. Schooling, alas, became neglected as soccer ability blossomed. At twelve years of age he was playing for a local district team, all of whose other players were much older than he, and at thirteen he was selected for a national school team. His all-consuming ambition at this time was to play for Scotland's senior team.

Meanwhile his father's health continued to deteriorate, and godly Mrs Stewart looked on with anguish, having sincerely dedicated all her children to the Lord and his service. One thing only mattered for her - being fully committed to the Lord Jesus Christ. She now prayed as never before for her boy who was being dazzled by the prospects of football fame. Concurrently, a breath from heaven was being felt in Glasgow as one evangelistic effort succeeded another. The mid-twenties in Britain were days of depression, culminating in the General Strike of 1926, and an industrial city like Glasgow suffered more than most. But God's people busied themselves with the work of the gospel and souls were converted in substantial numbers. Along with other young people, David, the oldest Stewart son, was converted and this combined with the general evangelistic atmosphere and his mother's prayers to surround James with a holy influence and testimony, of which he became increasingly conscious.

The crisis for the young footballer began in an evangelistic mission at which the Irish evangelist Tom Rea was preaching. James had heard many such evangelists - his mother had seen to this - but now under the ministry of Mr Rea the boy footballer knew he had reached a crossroads. The inward tussle continued for several nights, with the dizzy heights of football beckoning on one hand and the call of God on the other. For him the two could not go together; worldliness and godliness did not run hand-in-hand in the 1920s as they often do in the 1980s.

Capitulation came on the football field itself. Playing in a schoolboy championship match, young James could struggle no longer and during the game he cried to the Lord and knew that he was heard. Soon he was hurrying to tell his mother, 'I'm saved, I'm saved.' Delighted as she was, there was no surprise; she already had been assured that her boy would soon be converted, and conversion for her and for her son meant the end of football and the beginning of a life to be lived for God and for the gospel. A new day had dawned for young Jimmy Stewart, who was barely fourteen at the time.

Shortly afterwards, his father's struggle with ill health ended in early death, but not before he had heard James confessing Christ at a street meeting. No one had told the new convert to go out to witness and testify; it was in fact the normal thing to do in those Glasgow days but for James Stewart it was the first tentative step on the path which was to take him into a life of evangelism in native and foreign fields.

Since his mother was now a widow, James' remaining schooldays were short-lived, and before reaching fifteen he began work as a delivery boy for a grocer's shop, no other employment being possible for a lad with inadequate education and no formal training. But where football had once dominated his life, now it was Christ. He may not have sung Wesley's words, 'My heart is full of Christ and longs its glorious matter to declare,' but they perfectly express what was now true of him. The boy footballer became the boy preacher. Delivering groceries was an opportunity to deliver the gospel on the doorsteps. Sunday Schools, open-air meetings on street corners, outside football stadia, in fact in any place where people could be reached - there the boy preacher would take up his stand and proclaim Christ. If his schooling had been sparse, his knowledge of the Bible was comparatively extensive, the fruit of faithful Bible reading and teaching at home and church. Ere long he had become a familiar sight on Glasgow's streets, as he carried text-boards, handed out tracts and testified to all who stopped to listen.

Delivering groceries gave way to a job in a clothing factory at which over 1,000 people were employed. James' work was pressing new garments and soon he was earning bonuses for efficiency and speed. This did not prevent his witnessing within the factory, or singing hymns as he pressed the garments, all of which resulted in his being labelled 'daft Jimmy'.

His evenings were now spent in study at home or in one evangelistic effort or other which, together with long hours on the factory floor, began to undermine his health. This was eventually noticed by a director of the factory who suggested he should curtail his religious activities and concentrate on his daily work, in which he would certainly prosper. What was not possible was continuing to do both. The director insisted on a decision, a fact which forced James to make up his mind that, come what may, he would devote his life to preaching and evangelistic work.

Now eighteen and without a job, he prayed much for guidance and was led to write to James Bryant of the Open Air Mission, whom he had met a few months previously during a family holiday in Northern Ireland. Bryant and his co-worker lived in a 'gospel van' and travelled widely, preaching wherever they could. Young James had spent some time with them and Bryant had encouraged him to think he could be used in the same work. On hearing from James, Bryant persuaded the Open Air Mission to take on the young Scot as a full-time worker and because of his strong accent he was assigned to work with ex-police-sergeant Wheeler, initially in the lovely Borders area of southern Scotland. Life with 'Sergeant' Wheeler was disciplined, involving routine menial tasks as well as open-air preaching and witnessing.

After a period among the rural towns and villages of the Borders, Wheeler and his assistant moved on to other parts, in fact to any place where people could be reached with the gospel. One such place was Clydebank's docks and shipbuilding yards, where they preached to the workmen as they emerged through the gates after completing their day's work. The evangelist's efforts here were linked with missions conducted by the renowned W. P. Nicholson. A few years previously, Nicholson had been greatly used in revival in Northern Ireland and the time with him, during the Clydebank missions, left a deep impression upon James Stewart, who was still only twenty years of age.

In later years Stewart was to recall how Tom Rea, 'Sergeant' Wheeler and W. P. Nicholson had each taught him things in the work of evangelism which were to prove invaluable in places and conditions far removed from Scotland. Rea had seen much fruit in his campaigns in Northern Ireland and Scotland; Wheeler was the mature open-air evangelist, while Nicholson had experienced at first-hand the fires of revival. James Stewart profited from all three.

Once more providence intervened to redirect James' young life. A sustained period of overwork, during which he was preaching about forty times a week in the open air, began again to undermine his health and a rest was indicated. Extended leave enabled him to spend some time in the rural Borders country, and then he travelled to London, where he was soon speaking in Hyde Park and on Tower Hill. Here too he was gaining experience which would stand him in good stead in time to come.

While he was in London, he sought out Herbert White, who had founded an orphanage in South Woodford. James had met Mr White some time before and had been profoundly impressed with him and what he had heard of his work for orphaned children, which owed much to the way the famed George Müller had carried on the same work in Bristol. But Herbert White was also active in evangelistic witness and had a horse-drawn caravan, with which he reached out into Essex villages. James Stewart joined him in this effort and it was during this time in East Anglia that he began to be exercised in mind and heart for the peoples of eastern Europe. Voicing this growing concern on one occasion during breakfast at the orphanage, he was told by the godly matron to give himself to the task he was already doing and to forget the fanciful ideas he had just aired.

A further term of holding missions in widely scattered areas followed. He was accompanied by William McEwan, whose singing drew large crowds. The partnership was, however, comparatively short-lived and James continued on his own in the north-eastern counties of England. While there, he had an exceptional experience of the Lord and his infinite love: 'I was spending some time in prayer at bedtime when suddenly the heavens opened and I was given a glorious sense of the divine presence. Waves of divine love flooded my soul and I was overwhelmed by a manifestation of the Lord which made me weep with joy. For about three hours I enjoyed sweet communion with my blessed Lord - my Beloved had brought me into his banqueting house and his banner over me was love.'

This was how James was to speak of this experience in after years: 'I had felt some anointing of the Spirit on occasions before but this was something different.' Apart from anything else, it was for him a confirmation of a step he had taken to shun popular evangelism as it was then developing.

It was in the course of this itinerant evangelism that James Stewart met two young men from the Continent. While attending a

Text Carriers' convention in Liverpool, he met Oswald Blumit, a young Latvian who was then studying at Spurgeon's College in London. Blumit spoke of the great need of Latvia and other areas of eastern Europe and his profound burden and fervent spirit in prayer were undoubtedly a means used by God to point the young Scot to Latvia and regions beyond.

James also met another man from Europe, Enoch Wangberg from north Norway, who was studying at Glasgow's Bible Training Institute. Wangberg's father was a missionary among the Lapps in the 'land of the midnight sun' and Enoch's concern for the nomadic Lapps was no whit less than Blumit's for the Latvians. The two students left a deep impression on James: 'I realized that just across the English channel lay a veritable mission-field for whom nobody seemed to care.' These were his own words and he determined that if the Lord should call him to those multitudes he would surely go.

It was while he was conducting a mission on the Isle of Stronsay in the Orkney Islands that he felt that call. Walking along the shore one morning, face to the wind, he knew the Lord was bidding him to set that face towards eastern Europe and that he should begin in Riga, the capital of Latvia. This was early in the winter of 1934 and soon James was on his way homewards to tell his mother and family. He was barely twenty-four years of age, had no human backing, spoke no language other than English and had had no formal training for missionary work. Not surprisingly, his family and friends sought to dissuade him, but without success. But he did ask the Lord to confirm the call, and his prayer was unmistakably answered at a Saturday evening meeting in the curiously named Tent Hall in Glasgow.

Following D. L. Moody's great campaigns in Scotland, regular meetings continued in a large tent in Glasgow and the 'Tent' became an evangelistic centre. Eventually a large auditorium was built but the 'Tent' and its work were so firmly established that the label 'Tent' could not be dropped. Hence the name 'Tent Hall' was popularly adopted and, among other valued ministries, its Saturday night rallies regularly attracted over 2,000 people for many years.

The visiting speaker on that particular Saturday evening in 1934 was a missionary from South America, who suddenly, and entirely out of context, asserted that God was calling some young man in the meeting to serve him in foreign lands. James was sitting in the gallery and he knew beyond all doubt that he was the young man in question.

Without delay or any of the ado normally associated with the departure of a missionary for foreign fields - committees, valedictories, farewells etc. - James set out for Riga. It was the heart of winter, and as the journey progressed to the north-east the cold grew more severe. It was not surprising that by the time he arrived in Riga some days later, he was all but overcome with fatigue, hunger and temperatures well below freezing. He was, however, fortified by the inner conviction that it was the Lord who had brought him there, but neither he nor anyone else could have foreseen or planned the work that was now to begin - still less the blessing which was to follow.

Pastor William Fetler wrote in later years about the crowds which had packed Salvation Temple night after night as revival fires burned for weeks on end. It was he who had translated for the young Scots preacher, but he was also to prove a vital link in that he was familiar with the situations in other countries of eastern Europe to which James Stewart was soon to move.

3.
Revival in eastern Europe

Reports of James Stewart's work in the years leading up to World War II were often fragmentary and sometimes confused. It could hardly have been otherwise, especially at the outset, when no systematic account was kept and only snippets of news from letters he sent home became known among family and friends who prayed for him. The record has now been put straight by Mrs Ruth Stewart (now Mrs Fajfr) in her book *James Stewart, Missionary,* written after her husband's death. We can therefore trace the main features of his movements with confidence, though not with much detail.

Leaving the Baltic republics some time in 1935, James made his way southwards to Poland, where his first call was at the Warsaw headquarters of the Russian Missionary Society (RMS). This had been founded by William Fetler for the encouragement and support of native evangelists serving as they could in several countries of Eastern Europe. Some of these men had received a measure of training from Fetler himself, but others were farmers and artisans who laboured in evangelism as time and means permitted. All were men of faith and self-denial and James Stewart was not slow to share their zeal and efforts. Some of them were in touch with like-minded brethren within Russia, not very far away in terms of kilometres but generally isolated from fellowship. James helped the Polish brethren to take Bibles over the border to their Russian fellow-believers, who were maintaining the faith despite every official attempt, subtle and coarse, to stamp it out.

It was about this time that James received the first of many consignments of Scripture portions from the Scripture Gift Mission (SGM) in London which were to prove a great help to him in the years ahead. The distribution of these portions in the towns and villages of eastern Poland was afterwards made easier by the arrival of Douglas Stewart, James' younger brother, who at seventeen years of age was plunged into scenes and situations from which many older people would have shrunk.

Co-operation with the RMS evangelists led to meetings in theatres and public halls, their own scattered 'houses of prayer' being far too small to accommodate all the people. Writing to F. J. Miles, the RMS secretary in London, James described the blessing attending these efforts in Poland as even greater than what he had witnessed in Riga and Tallinn. Missions held in country towns along Poland's border with Russia were attended by overflowing crowds and none could say who or how many professed faith in Christ. When we remember that, like the Baltic states, a large chunk of eastern Poland was annexed by the Russians at the beginning of the war, we may well conclude that God graciously used James Stewart and those who toiled with him to prepare and fortify his people for what was soon to overtake them under the Communist regime.

It is fascinating to note that James was able to hold meetings among Jewish communities during those days. They had no hymns to sing and no Scriptures were available for distribution, but the gospel was preached through an interpreter and a few among them were converted. One Jewish woman had set out for the local cinema expecting to see a film starring James Stewart, the famous American actor. The name was on a poster outside the cinema! She was in the wrong place, however, and what she heard was James Stewart the evangelist preaching the gospel of Christ, something she had never heard before. She returned again and again until she was converted, to be followed soon by her Jewish husband. Alas, it was not long before the Nazis came and the Jews of Poland were swallowed up in their hideous anti-semitism.

It is always heartening to hear of God's faithful people in small and scattered groups, almost entirely unknown and certainly unsung, who yet witness a good confession in the most lonely situations. There were such groups in pre-war Poland, some of whom traced their origins to local people who had worked for a time in the West and had been found of him who saves sinners. Returning to their native land, they brought their new-found faith with them, together with Bibles and Gospel portions, and God used them to call out a remnant for himself.

An earlier missionary in eastern Poland, S. K. Hine, who translated the hymn 'How great thou art!', recounts how he met a few believers in this lonely region who were the fruit of a remarkable overruling providence. In 1915, when Tsarist troops were hastily retreating from the place, one of the soldiers unwittingly left his Bible behind. This remained a closed book for nearly twenty years because no one in the village could read. Then in 1934 a young woman who had learnt to read was handed the Bible. Haltingly she began to share her reading with neighbours, who were so moved with what they heard that several were converted, and these formed one of the small but sturdy companies of believers who were upholding the truth in the late 1930s and, we believe, subsequently within the embrace of the Russian bear. They would surely have lifted their voices and souls to sing, 'How great thou art!'

Precisely how long James Stewart was in the Baltic countries and then in Poland is not really clear. A visit to Holland was made from Riga but nothing of that trip has been reported. We know the main meetings in Riga lasted five months and there were other missions in Latvia and Estonia. He then spent some months in Poland, and towards the end of that time, while he was in Warsaw, he received an invitation to Czechoslovakia. The man who brought the invitation was Zdenek Koukol, who was a chocolate manufacturer and a Christian. James had already been feeling that it was time for him to move on and Czechoslovakia had been much in his thoughts and prayers. The invitation therefore came as no surprise to him and he had no difficulty in accepting it without delay.

It was now 1936 and meetings began in a church in Kutna Hora, the town not far from the capital Prague where Mr Koukol lived. If immediate success was anticipated it did not materialize. The meetings were cold and the Czechs unmoved, and after some days James Stewart was disappointed and confused. He began to wonder if he had made a mistake in leaving Poland, where there was fervency and joy, and he was even inclined to return there. However, Mr Koukol was convinced God would bless the work and he persuaded James to carry on. Meetings were arranged for the town of Kolin, where a large public hall was available, and local Christians gave themselves to earnest prayer. There was confession of sin too among the Christians and soon the blessing came as God's presence was made powerfully real and many sinners trusted Christ for salvation.

In Kolin a pattern was established which was subsequently followed by James Stewart wherever possible. Christians were called upon to pray for revival, and James ministered to them in morning meetings and joined them in visiting houses to extend invitations to the public meetings, which were soon to commence, and to distribute Scripture portions. Often the prayers were heard and meetings arranged for evangelistic outreach merged into scenes of revival, with the blessing continuing long after the evangelistic meetings had ended.

The work in Kutna Hora and Kolin extended first to Prague and then to Brno, and lasting fruit was gathered in both places. In Brno particularly, young people were converted in substantial numbers and went on to hold evangelistic meetings on their own long after James Stewart's ministry among them had ceased. Over two years later, Czechoslovakia fell to the Nazis and many of Hitler's forces were stationed in Brno - every fifth person in Brno at that time was said to be a German soldier, Even so, the young Christians maintained their evangelistic work in hospitals, schools and prisons and they also held meetings in homes in the surrounding villages. When some of their number were pressed into service in German war factories, their fellow believers at home sent food parcels which helped to keep them from starvation. Thus the blessing which fell on the Stewart meetings continued under the Nazi regime and beyond.

The pagan regimes of Babylon and Persia failed to destroy the faith of God's people. The Roman Caesars and others have likewise failed and Communism and every other 'ism' will finally have no greater success.

> Like a mighty army
> Moves the church of God.
> Brothers, we are treading
> Where the saints have trod.

Of all the countries in which James Stewart laboured in the late 1930s, none saw greater spiritual profit than Hungary. Unlike the other countries, Hungary had a comparatively strong Protestant tradition through its Reformed Church, which claimed twenty per cent of the population and which included an evangelical section. There were also other groups and movements embracing evangelical believers, one of whom was Dr Csia, who was the chief physician for the Hungarian Railways and a keen man of God. It was he who invited James Stewart to Budapest and as the latter arrived rather suddenly, meetings were arranged at short notice in a small Methodist 'Prayer Hall'.

The pattern begun in Czechoslovakia was now repeated, with meetings for prayer where James exhorted the believers to call upon God for revival and endeavoured to strengthen their faith and prayer by telling them what God had done in history and something of what he had been doing recently in the Baltic, Poland and Czechoslovakia. After two days the meetings moved to a larger Baptist church and for the second week a Reformed church seating 2,000 became the venue. Soon, sinners were being saved, prayer meetings were multiplied, and morning meetings for Christians began when James taught the Word and emphasized holiness of life and faithfulness in prayer and service - in short, Christian discipleship.

One statement James made at this time was that in Hungary, 'The free grace of the gospel is presented to sinners but the standard of discipleship has been omitted.' After a further period of meetings held in Budapest's largest concert hall, which was again overcrowded, invitations for meetings in other parts of the country were accepted, including the famed city of Debrecen near the Rumanian border, whose museum housed the original *'Ecce Homo'* painting. Debrecen was also widely known as the Geneva of Hungary because of its strong Reformed Church and Calvinist university. However, its theology was more intellectual than experimental, and it was said to be the hardest place in all Hungary so far as vital Christianity was concerned.

Right from the outset exceptional interest was kindled by Stewart's visit and the meetings flourished even more than in Budapest. By this time a converted Jew had become James' interpreter. Several able and godly men had interpreted in various places, but once Aladar Ungar had done so James was reluctant to

James Stewart addresses the young people's gathering at the 'Tattershall'.

use anyone else, Besides sharing the same desire for the gospel and for lost souls, Ungar and James were of one heart, so that the interpreter actually entered into the preaching itself.

Henceforth Ungar became a valuable member of the team in Hungary, though not without some opposition. Some people had been influenced by Nazi propaganda and they objected to a Jew taking part in the meetings. There were not only threatening letters, but one of the early meetings in Debrecen was interrupted by a demonstration against Ungar. However, these hiccups were soon overcome, and the meetings which followed were among the most amazing seen in any country. As in every place, the preaching was direct and uncomplicated; the great evangelistic verses were expounded and applied with simplicity and due sobriety, and the swelling multitudes could not have enough. Debrecen's local newspapers reported six meetings being held each day, the first at seven in the morning and the last at nine-thirty at night. It was estimated that 4,000 people attended the seven o'clock meeting every evening throughout the mission.

'Only in Debrecen', James Stewart was to say later, 'have I seen people running through the streets to attend the last meeting of the day, held in a YMCA where they prayed for the revival to continue and for unsaved loved ones, while some would spontaneously testify to what the Lord had done for their souls.' After the final meeting of the mission had ended, hundreds in the congregation wept copiously, while hundreds more turned homewards, singing God's praises in the streets as they went. Four months later, over 200 men and women were meeting for prayer every morning and about 700 attended a similar meeting on a Monday evening, and in the meantime an overspill into the surrounding villages had taken place as peasant farmers and their families hungered for the word of life. Many of these were Roman Catholics who heard the one true gospel for the first time.

James Stewart returned to Budapest in April 1938 when the political atmosphere was becoming increasingly tense as war-clouds gathered over Czechoslovakia and Hungary. On this occasion the meetings were held in a large indoor riding school known as the Tattershall. A small army of helpers was marshalled to set out the chairs before each evening meeting and to stack them away afterwards so that the arena would be clear for the riding school the

A weekday meeting in Debrecen

following morning. Though it was April, the weather was cold and the large building very draughty. James preached with his overcoat on and the people brought blankets to keep them warm while listening attentively to the preaching. Much prayer was made for a change in the weather, and change it did, and thousands came night after night for two weeks in the Tattershall and for a further week in another large hall. The work begun at this time continued in various parts of Hungary until the outbreak of war in September 1939 as those who had been revived and others, who had been awakened and saved, took the gospel to those still in darkness and the shadow of death. Dr Csia, who had first invited James Stewart to Hungary, said that after the evangelist had left many Protestant pastors continued in the work of revival which had come to their churches and elsewhere.

James was back in Hungary in 1939 and again in 1940 when war had blacked out Europe and general mobilization had taken place. He preached to thousands in a university courtyard in total darkness, as black-out was complete, his text being John 19:41. Though he could not see the people he could hear them weeping profusely. Even when he returned to Budapest in 1946, before the Iron Curtain fell, he found evidence of continuing revival among the believers despite what they and others had suffered in and through the fires of war.

Besides being the scene of powerful revival, with meetings thronged with vast crowds, Hungary, and its capital Budapest in particular, was to bring a new dimension into James Stewart's life and work. He was now nearly twenty-seven and his life had hitherto been totally given to evangelism. But in Budapest he met Ruth Mahan, who was a Baptist missionary from the U.S.A., in charge of a Bible School for girls in the city. Ruth had been active in some of James' missions and was startled to receive a proposal of marriage from him just a few short days after their first meeting. They were married in the hall of the Scots Mission to the Jews where Professor John (Rabbi) Duncan had laboured. The best man was their dear Ungar and the guest of honour was James' mother, all the way from Glasgow. Henceforth James and Ruth were to work together in Europe and America, Ruth invariably at her husband's side. She was eminently qualified to help in meetings for women and young people and to deal competently with the correspondence which was rapidly mounting as news of what was happening in eastern Europe spread first in Britain and Ireland and then in the U.S.A.

4. Random reports

Neither the purpose nor the scope of this present work permits anything like a comprehensive account of the extensive activities of James Stewart and his colleagues in the years preceding World War II. By the time James and Ruth Stewart were married a team of five, including James, Ruth, Douglas Stewart and Dr and Mrs Neighbour from the U.S.A., were involved in public meetings, house visitation, Scripture distribution, Bible training courses and other activities, and through them many native evangelists in several countries were being helped in various ways. James had also visited and preached in other countries - Yugoslavia, Bulgaria, Holland, Greece - and had attended conventions and other meetings in Scotland, Ireland and Wales. Following 1938 he and Ruth were in Yugoslavia, Bulgaria, Rumania and Czechoslovakia up to 1940, when the exigencies of war forced them to leave Europe and they made their home in Asheville, North Carolina, which was Ruth's home town.

Not the least remarkable aspect of the story is that so many countries, with their diverse ethnic groups, were included in their labours - Latvians, Estonians, Russians, Poles, Czechs, Magyars, Serbs, Croats, Bulgars, to name the main groups. The social spectrum of the people affected was equally wide-ranging - young and old, city-dwellers and peasants, prominent people and obscure, educated and illiterate, rich and poor, were all numbered among those who were saved and revived. A few abbreviated testimonies and reports are worth quoting, not only to demonstrate the relevance of the gospel of grace to people of all classes but even more, for the glory of God, whose work it all was.

One of Poland's evangelical pastors reported that 'The meetings in many places gathered thousands of Poles, Russians and Ukrainians and resulted in many of them trusting Christ.' Mr Assen Simeonoff, evangelical representative to the Crown in Bulgaria, said that meetings in his country were 'crowded every night and the Spirit of God worked mightily. Hundreds of souls accepted Christ as their Saviour.'

Events in Hungary were seen thus by Professor Kis of Budapest University, himself an outstanding evangelical Christian: 'Our unbelief was greatly strengthened when this young man, simple in dress and demeanour, arrived. We were confident the little hall we had booked would be sufficient but we were disillusioned when the Holy Spirit began to work. It soon became evident that our prayer life was poor and our obedience and sacrifice only partial...Our Prime Minister personally gave instructions to the Police Chief that he must in no way hinder the meetings.' Another report from Hungary said that 'More than 3,000 souls have come to know the saving power of the precious blood of Christ. No sensational methods have been used; the gospel has been simply preached in the power of the Holy Spirit.'

Among those Hungarian converts was a labourer who testified: 'I was brought up in the darkness of Roman Catholicism but through the meetings in Debrecen I have come to know Jesus Christ as my Saviour. The change in my life is remarkable: we have a new home and the Bible is my constant companion and prayer my heart's desire.' A Jewish doctor in Hungary testified that 'God has done wonderful things for us. Out of curiosity I followed the crowds to the meetings and was immediately gripped. Night after night I groped for light and I am glad now to confess that the Lord Jesus Christ is the Son of God and my Saviour. At the meetings I met a Jewish lady who had also been saved and now the Lord has shown it is his will for us to marry and to work together for him.'

Writing to James Stewart, a Hungarian pastor stated that 'The past few weeks have been the greatest in my life. My two sons who were careless and without Christ, having for years rejected the offer of God's mercy, attended the meetings night after night and are today valiantly witnessing for Christ.'

Ruth Stewart in 1947 with children, Jimmy (2yrs)
and Sheila (7yrs).

James and Douglas Stewart between them had paid nine visits to Brno in Czechoslovakia where the power of the Spirit was much in evidence. Preaching in the local prison, James had taken the conversion of the Philippian jailer as his theme. One prisoner who was converted said, 'The Son of God has snapped the fetters of sin that bound me and set me gloriously free.' Three sisters living in a village near Brno read in the local newspaper about the first meetings being held in the city. Their dearly loved father had recently died and their grief had not been relieved by repeated cinema and theatre visits. 'We can never forget that night when, with many others, we passed from death to life,' they wrote later, going on to say, 'This happened eighteen months ago since when we have been maintaining a witness in our village.'

During those first meetings in Brno a civil engineer and his wife were converted. A few months later, through the third series of meetings in the city, their two adult sons came to a saving knowledge of Christ. On his way to Brno on one occasion James had stopped at a small town and preached for twenty minutes in the open air to a large crowd which had gathered, Roman Catholics to a man. Having a day to spare before starting in Brno he preached three times in Stara Tura, with hundreds present at each meeting, many of them in picturesque national costume. Meetings were frequently held in this way in scattered places without prior notice and salvation in Christ was preached to large crowds who assembled spontaneously. Another report in Czechoslovakia said that 'Halls were crowded with people of all ages in Bohemia, Moravia and Slovakia, and hundreds have testified to their faith in Christ, while the hearts of believers have been revived.' A German magazine carried a report by some Bible School students: 'We crossed the frontier to Nachod [in Czechoslovakia] and attended meetings in a theatre [conducted by James Stewart]. Roman Catholics, free-thinkers and all classes were present and heard simple but effective preaching of the gospel and many turned to Christ.'

A significant feature of the work was the fact that the breath of spiritual power so evident in the ministry of the Stewart brothers also manifested itself in that of some of the native evangelists who were associated with them. A Latvian named Oscar Abers, having been provided with a motorcycle, was holding cottage meetings in remote areas of his native land. These were often so crowded 'that the oil-lamps were almost snuffed out for want of air'. At a meeting held in a hired hall in a strongly Roman Catholic town, over 500 people were listening to the message when two priests jumped onto the platform and ordered all the Catholics to leave at once. There was a hurried scramble for the doors and some even clambered out through the windows! Even so, the young preacher had the joy of 'leading precious souls to the Lord Jesus'. One native evangelist preached at the opening of a 'prayer house' in the isolated heart of Moravia. Meetings went on for four days and 'Souls were brought to the Lord as God poured out his blessing upon us.'

One rather quaint development in Hungary saw a pastor, Emil Bretz, acquiring an old horse-drawn bus from the Budapest local authority and using it to travel to surrounding country districts to preach the gospel. Bretz and his helpers slept in the old bus at night and used it in the day as a pulpit for open-air meetings and as a bookstall, for selling Bibles and other literature. The meetings often continued after nightfall, when antique carbide lamps provided a dim and fading light. Wherever possible the final meeting would be held in a Protestant church in order to link converts and hearers to the only available local church. Then, with borrowed horses, the bus-turned-gospel-van was hauled away to the next village venue.

Space forbids us to recount many other tokens of the blessings on the varied work but we must note one other venture, both for its own sake and for its implications. Given the background of the prevailing evangelical dearth in each country, many of the native evangelists who helped the Stewart work and who, in turn, were helped in their own ministries, were of limited education and theological understanding. This prompted James Stewart to arrange short-term Bible courses for their benefit and several of these were held in more than one country. One was held in Poland in May 1939 when nearly fifty men attended, some of whom had laboriously travelled long distances in order to be present. The subjects set for the course included repentance, justification by faith, grace and the Holy Spirit. The books of Acts and Romans were also studied, as were the lives and works of C. H. Spurgeon and Hudson Taylor.

The train fares of those who had travelled long distances were reimbursed as none of them could boast much of this world's goods.

One brother arrived late and explained that he had waited for a calf to be born, so that he could sell it to pay his fare! Others came on bicycles, one having cycled 100 kilometres. When asked if he was tired he replied that the Lord had given him a strong tail wind which had made the journey easy! All the students brought sacks which were filled with straw to provide mattresses on which they were content to sleep each night. Their joy and profit may have been clouded by what was then going on around them. Mobilization had already begun in Poland as Germany amassed her armies to the west and Russia prepared hers to the east. But the fellowship and ministry of the course would also have fortified them to maintain the faith through the dark years ahead. The whole course cost £140, money truly well spent.

These are just a few extracts from piecemeal reports which filtered through in letters and occasional factual accounts. They indicate surely that unusual blessing attended the ministry of James Stewart and those who served with him in eastern Europe in the late 1930s. So far we have just seen a broad outline of the origin and growth of James Stewart's evangelistic work up to the commencement of hostilities in 1939, and the blessing which accompanied it in the revival of believers and the conversion of sinners in very considerable numbers. Before we follow the story further, reference must be made to some of the practical steps which were taken at this time and which were to have consequences far in excess of anything that was then foreseen.

When he left Glasgow for Riga in 1934 James Stewart had given the names of a few interested friends to his elder brother David, and for the next two years a trickle of reports was circulated among these supporters in Scotland and further afield, with the result that gifts had been forthcoming which were channelled to James for his own maintenance and for the work generally. Eventually James came home to speak in various centres, and consequently further gifts flowed in to the Stewart home in Glasgow. David Stewart was still living at home and, probably without realizing it, he became both secretary and treasurer of the developing enterprise. When Douglas joined James and as a growing number of local evangelists and colporteurs became involved, the needs increased. Scripture portions and tracts in the various languages were received from the Scripture Gift Mission in London, but these had to be augmented by repeated printings. In addition, financial assistance was given to secure or build 'prayer houses' - mission halls, as we would call them - where Christians and converts could meet in places where no other churches were available. All the campaigns in the cities and towns were financed by the local Christians and there were some comparatively generous gifts, but the overall demands of the growing work meant that help was needed from Britain. However, with the coming of Ruth Stewart and Dr Neighbour their friends and contacts in the U.S.A. also began to lend support, all of which under God's good hand met every requirement as it emerged. An incipient missionary society was thus developing which, it was confidently expected, would soon become a powerful evangelistic force throughout Europe. The reality was rather different, at least in its outworking, though not in its ultimate goal.

5.
A time of war

It is not surprising that the conspicuous blessing which had attended five years' evangelistic labours in several countries should have inspired those who shared in it to hope for a 'new day' in the cause of the gospel in Europe. But the day which actually dawned was vastly different, though not entirely unforeseen. James Stewart wrote in February 1938, 'Nothing will save Europe from bloodshed and war save a Holy Ghost awakening,' and he went on to plead with Christians on the Continent, in Britain and the U.S.A. to pray fervently for such an awakening. The prospect of war lent urgency to all efforts to spread the gospel, and this was expressed in what became something of a slogan for the work: 'Waging a warfare of aggressive evangelism among Europe's millions.'

Throughout the late 1930s Adolf Hitler's Germany had been accumulating arms and manoeuvring for a major conflict, as had Soviet Russia, while the nations of the west had largely slumbered in wishful thinking and apathy. Under the pretext of *Lebensraum* ('living space') Hitler had annexed Austria, then the Sudetenland, which had been a province of Czechoslovakia, where many Germans lived, before finally invading Poland in 1939. In the meantime, Russia had thrust her superiority on Finland and then occupied the tiny Baltic States before invading Poland from the east.

By 1940 all the countries of eastern Europe had either been overrun by invading armies, or subjugated by a combination of threats and alliances, and almost the whole Continent was locked in

World War II. Soon the scarifying effects of blitzkriegs, blanket-bombings and scorched-earth policies were desolating large areas of Europe, reducing cities to mere rubble and sweeping multitudes of their people to eternity by sudden and violent death. Millions more were herded into concentration camps to languish, starve or else be liquidated, and eventually there were hordes of refugees and displaced persons being hounded from pillar to post by the remorseless exigencies of total war.

The high hopes and fervent prayer for revival in Europe were thus rudely dashed and silenced, and it must have been a harrowing experience for the Stewarts and their colleagues not only to see their plans in ruins, but also to have close relationships with so many of God's people in several countries abruptly and completely severed. The situation which had already seen so much blessing and which had held such rich promise of a still greater harvest of souls was catastrophically overturned and, in the event, would never be recovered.

While no attempt has been made to give here a comprehensive account of the Stewarts' work in eastern Europe up to the Second World War, we have traced its more prominent features, sufficiently I trust to uncover those roots from which the European Missionary Fellowship eventually stemmed. Before we pursue the story further, we need to consider, if only briefly, the ethos and the principles which characterized James Stewart and his ministry, some of which continue in the EMF today.

As we have seen, neither of the Stewart brothers received formal theological training and they knew nothing of ministerial recognition or even sponsorship by any evangelical society. It is indeed almost certain that, like so many before and after them, they would have been rejected by an established missionary society because they lacked the educational requirements normally assumed to be essential. In this sense, at least in part, they could be likened to those first evangelists of old who were described by their enemies as 'unlearned and ignorant men'. But it could also be said of them that 'they had been with Jesus', having been nurtured in evangelical faith and practice by godly parents who had abundantly proved that faith in harsh daily experience - a faith and practice founded on love for Christ and obedience to God's Word.

The Stewarts' father had died in comparatively early years after a long illness which had brought poverty and privation to the family. Their mother, though widowed, was diligent in prayer and the family's straitened circumstances were not allowed to hinder Bible instruction or worship around the hearth. Her rich reward on earth was to see her children converted, with two of them serving the Lord in foreign lands and a third busily occupied at home in what became to all intents and purposes a mission office. Whatever else they lacked, therefore, the Stewart brothers had heard the Scriptures taught consistently and had seen in their own home life lived in accordance with scriptural principles, and this in some real measure prepared them for their future. Further, their Christian life and activity had been within the fervent evangelical ethos of Glasgow, the supreme thrust of which was to win lost men and women for Christ - 'by all means save some' being the order of the day. This had undoubtedly influenced James Stewart in his early days as a young believer and, together with his own ability and venturesome zeal, had moved him to take up evangelistic witness with a confidence which many in other circumstances would find surprising.

The Bible Training Institute was an essential part of the Glasgow evangelical scene in the 1920s, but there was apparently no suggestion that either James or Douglas should attend there. It was in any case unlikely that James would have been accepted for the BTI or any other college until his late teen years, and by then he was deeply entrenched in evangelistic activity with a spiritual maturity beyond his years. It is clear too that James was a student all his life, a fact which enabled him to grasp prevailing theological and practical issues. His lifelong emphases, however, were evangelism and revival. Everything else had to be subservient to these two crucial needs, which for him were inseparable.

None the less it cannot be doubted that James Stewart valued Bible training as preparation for missionary service. He counselled many prospective candidates to seek adequate training and, significantly, he arranged short-term courses for native evangelists and colporteurs whose educational opportunities had been severely limited. And this in turn led to plans for a full-scale Bible School in central Europe, plans which did not come to fruition because of war. But while he recognized the need for training, it must be emphasized that for James no amount of Bible knowledge and training could be a substitute for vital faith, a love for souls and the outpouring of the Holy Spirit's power. For him, to be taught and owned of God was more important than to be trained formally and sponsored by men, though he never considered that the one necessarily clashed with the other. One of his favourite quotations was 'Mine the mighty ordination of the nail-pierced hands', and it was his firm belief that this constituted the supreme qualification for all who would preach Christ to lost souls. In a later statement he described true evangelism as 'working in communion with the Holy Spirit' and this was surely what he had seen and known for five years in eastern Europe.

A very significant feature of his pre-war missions was the absence of high-pressure propaganda and of many of the evangelistic techniques which have become 'normal' in later times. The common practice was that a series of meetings would be announced, often at short notice and, in any case, without any elaborate organization or publicity. Wherever possible the services began with prayer meetings at which James Stewart invariably ministered to Christians, few though they often were, his purpose being to awaken and challenge them to pray and work earnestly for revival and for the salvation of sinners. Again and again, meetings begun in this way expanded rapidly, embracing men and women whose hearts had been moved and consciences smitten. And as the spiritual fires spread, unbelievers took notice and many came under conviction of sin and were saved.

The passion which animated the Stewarts and their fellow-workers throughout those years arose in part from the vision of countless souls in Europe without hope and without God. They believed without reservation that sinners without Christ are eternally lost and they were utterly convinced that God had called them to proclaim and offer freely to those European multitudes that salvation which is in Christ by faith alone, and they devoted themselves and all the resources available to them to this supreme task.

In the general evangelical climate of those years the place and function of the local church tended to be assumed rather than emphasized, possibly because extra-church evangelism, so prominent in post-war years, was not as yet all that widespread. Though little was published to indicate it at the time, James Stewart's work was frequently linked with a church, or churches, or local groups of believers which in effect, if not in name, were the 'gathered church'. It may not be true to say that all the Stewarts' activities were conjoined to local churches; there were areas where no churches existed, and many that did exist were Catholic or moribund and liberal Protestant. Even so, prayer meetings for Christians before the commencement of a campaign and for converts at the end of it were generally within the context of local churches and evangelical groups. As a result these local churches were strengthened spiritually and numerically in one country after another - the Baptists in Latvia, churches of the Russian Missionary Society in Poland, Brethren and other assemblies in Czechoslovakia and Hungary, and some Lutheran and Reformed churches too. It is also worth noting that the 'prayer houses', often in lonely regions, were in effect local branches of the church of Jesus Christ. The large evangelistic meetings were often held in public halls because church buildings could not accommodate the crowds, but these had frequently started in churches and were invariably closely related to churches and their leaders.

Another prominent feature in the Stewarts' work was the circulation of Bibles, New Testaments and Scripture portions, as well as other literature. From the first it had been seen that the Word of God was in short supply and much effort was devoted to meeting the need, though, with so many languages involved and resources so sparse, the task at times must have appeared well-nigh impossible. Besides substantial help received from various agencies, steps were taken to print Bibles, Scripture portions and literature, together with some of James Stewart's messages, and these were circulated in large quantities. Plans were also made to produce books on biblical doctrines and biographies but, like those for the Bible school, these were frustrated by the outbreak of the war.

Reference must also be made to another aspect of the Stewarts' ministry which was to prove vitally significant in post-war years. Though their efforts had been largely concentrated on eastern Europe, repeated contacts were made with evangelicals in countries of the west. It would seem almost inevitable that their first-hand knowledge and experience of the Roman and Orthodox Churches in the east should kindle concern for the Latin nations of southern Europe and for Greece. James Stewart was in Greece for meetings more than once during the years just before the war and he also visited Italy and Spain, among other western nations.

Reports of those visits reflected his acute awareness of the profound spiritual darkness prevailing in those countries and he often expressed the hope that some evangelistic work could be started in them in future years. In God's providence this proved to be the preparation for the day soon to dawn when eastern countries would be tightly closed and new fields in the west would be opened.

Looking back after half a century, we can trace the marked benefits resulting from the five years of ministry up to 1940 in three far-reaching ways. Firstly, there was the reviving and awakening of groups of believers, large and small, across many countries. Lonely and languishing Christians were challenged to give themselves to fervent prayer and witness among their kith and kin, while lost sinners in very considerable numbers were brought to saving faith in the Lord Jesus Christ. In short, evangelical religion was stirred and strengthened in exceptional measure under the blessing of God which, undoubtedly, accompanied the tireless efforts of the Stewarts and their colleagues.

Secondly, the scene of such blessing was shortly overrun by the holocaust of war. That the evangelical faith survived at all and continues today in those eastern lands is surely due, in God's providence, in no small part to those efforts which began in late 1934 and were maintained until the beginning of 1940. The links established with the believers in eastern Europe, especially the local evangelists and colporteurs, were preserved, albeit tenuously, during the war with the hope that co-operation could be resumed even more extensively when hostilities ended. When the Iron Curtain fell, these hopes evaporated almost overnight and those believers on its eastern side were perforce left to uphold the faith in the face of fierce opposition. Thanks be to God, many of them, together with their spiritual children, are still doing so. It is not too much to believe that God raised up James and Ruth Stewart, Douglas and those native workers to help prepare his church in eastern Europe for the dark days of war and beyond.

Finally, though the harsh consequences of war shattered the plans and hopes for even greater efforts when hostilities ceased, what had been learnt was put to early and good use in western Europe and, subsequently, in other parts of the world. Several agencies for the spread of the gospel have stemmed from the work of the Stewarts and these continue today in Europe and further afield, among them the European Missionary Fellowship.

6.
A mission is set up

By the end of 1938 the Stewarts had formed a missionary organization under the name of the European Evangelistic Fellowship, with councils of reference and offices in Britain and the U.S.A. The British office was still the Stewart home in Glasgow in the care of David Stewart. Fuller reports of the work were duly published and a statement of accounts for 1939 showed that over £4,000 had been received and expended entirely on the field. Figures for SGM literature indicated that 5,000 New Testaments, 353,000 Gospels and 475,000 Scripture booklets had been distributed in seven countries.

A huge volume of work by native evangelists and colporteurs is reflected by these figures and it is evident that Douglas Stewart was prominent in this aspect of the work. Writing in 1939, when he was still only twenty years of age, he said he was in Poland and that he and eight Polish brethren were distributing Scriptures among Jews, Russians and Poles. Douglas continued these activities in Hungary until the outbreak of war, but in 1941 he was officially told to leave the country forthwith - no easy task seeing that most of Europe was now engulfed in hostilities. He trudged his way through Yugoslavia, hoping to escape to the west, but was eventually arrested by the Nazis and imprisoned as a spy for the duration of the war. Meanwhile, James and Ruth Stewart were to spend most of the war years in the U.S.A. Up until America's entry into the war late in 1941, they were able to send financial aid to those native colleagues they had been obliged to leave but, after Pearl Harbour, all contact was cut off. Eventually plans were laid and preparations made for an early return to Europe as soon as possible after the war ended. Those plans included an expansion of all the activities pursued in pre-war years, with British and American workers being sent to augment the national evangelists in the various countries.

To implement these plans the European Evangelistic Crusade (EEC) was formally constituted in the U.S.A. in 1944, with headquarters in Buffalo, New York State. The new title was adopted to avoid confusion with other societies and Buffalo was chosen because of its proximity to Canada, where much interest had been kindled through meetings which James and Ruth had been able to conduct there. Actually the first full-time EEC members in North America were Milton and Mary Lovering, Canadians from Toronto, who took charge of the Buffalo headquarters, which were to become a hive of activity as interest in Europe burgeoned among American evangelicals. They subsequently served in France although both were over fifty years old!

Developments were forthcoming in Britain too. The few people who had followed James Stewart with prayer and gifts had multiplied. David Stewart had been obliged to seek help and had found it in Ethel Kay, who had voluntarily lent a hand for a few years, before moving to Glasgow to work full-time. In 1945 a British branch of the EEC was established, with Miss Kay as secretary, and in 1946 new headquarters were established in St Leonards-on-Sea. A year later Betty Stevens, the first EEC British missionary, went to France, thereby becoming the forerunner of a team of workers which is still growing. Early in 1949 David Stewart had to relinquish his work as treasurer, after fifteen years of service willingly given, and Sam Reed of East London became Hon. Treasurer, a post he graced for nearly twenty years.

Later the same year the Rev. Donald Stuart, later to become Superintendent of the Grove Street Institute in Glasgow, became the EEC British Home Director, a step which duly led to the formation of an Executive Committee in 1950. Mr Stuart resigned in 1952 and was succeeded by the present writer.

These developing steps in Britain were paralleled by similar measures in Holland and Switzerland, where EEC branches were established. So in little more than four years a strong section had

The Rev. Donald Stuart, the EEC British Home Director, with James Stewart.

taken root in North America and comparatively smaller ones in three European countries, and a Field Director with his own office had been established in Switzerland; his name was Armin Hoppler, and in after years he became the international secretary of Scripture Union.

It needs to be said that these arrangements and their implications for gospel work in Europe were very largely due to the vision and energy of James Stewart, whose heart desire was to see a truly international body of workers, foreign and native, spreading the gospel of Christ among Europe's millions. He was, however, acutely conscious of the grim conditions which plagued Europe for a decade in the aftermath of war. The vast numbers of hungry and homeless refugees and displaced persons could not be ignored. Food and clothing parcels began to flow through EEC channels, first from the American section and then from the branches in Britain, Holland and Switzerland, to the teeming camps in several countries. Large quantities were eventually handled and a relief centre was set up by the Swiss EEC in addition to all the parcels sent direct by the other sections. The Swiss, as ever, were commendably thorough in the laborious work of cleaning, repairing, pressing and parcelling clothing, used and new, and all was done with love and joy for the succour and relief of the needy. But the camps and their occupants were viewed with spiritual eyes which meant that physical needs were not allowed to overshadow those of the soul. Relief parcels were invariably accompanied by Scripture portions in the appropriate languages and wherever possible were delivered personally by EEC missionaries and their helpers. Regular meetings for adults and children were held in many camps in Germany and Austria, and evangelistic missions were sometimes arranged which yielded fruit in many who had lost all in this world, finding life anew in Christ. When EEC missionaries Lee Reimer from Canada and Elisabeth Schmidt from Hungary were married in Austria, much of their honeymoon was spent in an Austrian refugee camp, where they held meetings which resulted in several conversions.

This work of relief-cum-evangelism continued in a few countries up to the end of the 1950s, by which time the face of western Europe was rapidly changing. America's unprecedented 'Marshall Plan' brought economic aid to the war-weary nations which sparked off a recovery of prosperity and thereby helped to heal the disfiguring wounds. Refugee camps closed with increasing pace as their occupants were absorbed into local communities or were accepted as immigrants in several countries of the world. Within what seems in retrospect a remarkably short space of time, normality with prosperity took over where suffering and despair had held sway and one important aspect of EEC work in the post-war period came to an end and the resources devoted to it were switched to the parallel ministry of evangelism which in the meantime had been growing apace.

It was nearly thirty years before a similar specific ministry of relief was undertaken by the European Missionary Fellowship (the British successor of the EEC). The scene on that occasion was Poland, where political strife and economic depression had brought on a severe scarcity of food, clothing and medicines. The plight of millions became an international crisis and many agencies in the west took up the task of rushing supplies into the country. By this time EMF had begun supporting Polish pastors and their churches in several parts of Poland and steps were taken to send supplies particularly to them and their fellow-believers. Some deliveries went to scattered groups of believers to the east of Warsaw and could well have catered for the needs of some who had heard James and Douglas Stewart preach almost fifty years before. This effort was of comparatively short duration as the crisis in Poland passed and the necessities of life became available again. The time may come for another effort of this kind to be made; it must, however, be no more than an adjunct. The chief work must always be that which concerns the souls of men and women and their crucial need for that 'gift of God [which] is eternal life through Jesus Christ our Lord'.

7.
West of the Iron Curtain

The beginning of 1946 had seen James Stewart back in Czechoslovakia, in the expectation that contact with all the national workers could soon be renewed, that the activities of pre-war days would be restarted and further projects would materialize. Large and fruitful meetings were held in Prague and in Brno, where successive halls became too small as great numbers flocked once more to hear the gospel. In fact, this was to be his last mission in the country. The mission ended, he went on to Hungary but was detained by the Communists and compelled to leave. Returning to Czechoslovakia, he found himself followed everywhere and to avoid bringing trouble on local Christians he left the country.

The late Jan Masaryk, Czechoslovakian Foreign Minister at the time and a Christian, told James that 'Only the gospel of Christ can save my country,' but as far as that crisis was concerned it was already too late. Within days the brave Masaryk died in circumstances fraught with suspicion of foul play and the country joined the other nations of the east behind the Iron Curtain.

Before the curtain finally fell, however, Douglas Stewart and his wife Sue, together with Steve and Helen Torbico, spent two years in Czechoslovakia until they too were obliged to leave in 1948. Douglas had been released from the concentration camp in 1945 in a poor state of health following nearly five years of privations and suffering. He subsequently played a prominent part in the growth of the EEC in America but his health remained

Flower-seller in Banska Bystrica, Czechoslovakia

impaired and he died in 1969 at the early age of fifty-two.

With eastern Europe closed to them, the Stewart brothers turned towards western Europe, since they were already familiar with many of its countries and the prevailing conditions there. The American EEC sent a growing number of missionaries, some of them of European stock and able to speak the languages of their forbears. Conditions in Germany and other parts at that time had to be seen to be believed. One of the first missionaries to Germany was Tina Blatz from Canada, and her first home, in which she lived for a year, was what had been the bathroom of a house which was otherwise gutted, this being the only shelter she could find in the city of Kassel. Widely-scattered communities had suffered on a scale beyond reckoning, if not by invasion and occupation then by blanket-bombing, so that few among them had not been grievously affected. Refugees and displaced persons posed massive problems, and their camps, overcrowded and often lacking elementary facilities, were scenes of moral degradation as well as physical misery.

Chaos also reigned for a time in civil and social realms, as political systems which had once appeared stable had either been destroyed or were in the melting-pot as a result of intrigues within or pressures from without.

It was into this kind of situation that EEC missionaries from U.S.A., Canada and Britain were sent, and they were glad to receive help from some native Christians and a few of their leaders. The dominating aim was evangelism by all possible means. Tents large and small were used in some countries, and missions were also held in established churches. Western Europe had become a vast mission-field and prevailing conditions made it one of pressing urgency. With the international scene so fluid and the future so uncertain, the overriding consideration was to proclaim the good news to the multitudes before it was too late.

The situation being what it was, we can understand why the task of founding and building up gospel churches was not generally pursued. This may seem strange with hindsight but at the time there were influencing factors which have to be taken into account. In the first place, the refugee camps were no places for founding churches. Life in them was so confused and insecure that anything solid and lasting was quite unreal. Further, rehabilitation, which began slowly and then gathered momentum, meant that even the most orderly of camps had no long-term future.

Even more significant was the widespread fear that opportunities for evangelism would not long remain. Although peace had been declared in Europe and the Far East, the reverberations of two atomic bombs in Japan still echoed in people's minds, if not in their ears, and the Continent in any case was split down the middle, dividing not only countries and cities, but communities and even families. Communism was threatening in the east and the Allies in the west were ready to resist, all of which meant that two well-heeled armies of unimaginable destructive potential were facing each other across contested frontiers. The overwhelming emotions of the times were tension, terror, grief and much despair.

For evangelicals, as for people in general, and not least for the EEC, it was a time of crisis, and this was reflected, perhaps unwittingly, in the mission's approach to evangelism. A few of the headlines in the published reports of those days were 'Christ or chaos', 'Europe is dying' and 'Five minutes to midnight', which may appear extravagant now, but not so then.

In such an atmosphere it is not surprising that the long-term aim of evangelism - church planting and building - tended to receive lip-service but little more. The vital task was to win souls for Christ; what became of them afterwards could not really be foreseen.

Within a few years the crisis was passing and people were regaining confidence and a sense of well-being. Strangely enough, the notorious 'Cold War' was bringing a kind of strained stability to the international scene - the deterrent was working. A new prosperity too was spreading across western Europe, banishing hardship and despair and eventually replacing them with materialism and complacency. Having feared the future, Europeans now felt that man can 'live by bread alone'. A new situation confronted all who were concerned for the souls of men and women.

Faced with western Europe, first in the post-war years of chaos and crisis, and then in renewed confidence and materialism, the forces of historic Christendom had little to offer men and women in either state. Romanism had played politics throughout the shifting fortunes of war, its chief concern being, as ever, to protect its monolithic structure and maintain its powerful sway. Whether to affirm its Mariolatry or to arrest its incipient decline, or both, the Roman church declared 1950 a 'Marian Year' and promulgated the Assumption of Mary as a dogma essential for salvation. But little ice was cut anywhere except among the 'faithful'; something more than gross superstition was required to meet the challenge of Europe in its recovery from the devastation of war.

Protestantism was if anything, in worse, straits, with almost all its branches in various stages of decline. Having largely succumbed to liberalism, it could only offer an admixture of man-centred religion and various forms and traditions. True, hope had begun to spring again for many in the rise of the World Council of Churches which, grotesquely as it now appears, was supposed to be the answer to militant Communism and humanism. Some initial excitement was generated but this did not last as it became evident that the materialistic multitudes remained unaffected. Twentieth-century Protestantism had largely lost its *raison d'etre* and had found nothing of substance to replace it. So far as the millions of western Europe were concerned, they could get along quite nicely without either Catholicism or Protestantism.

Yet the doors were already wide open in many of the countries and were slowly being forced open in the traditional Catholic strongholds of Italy, Spain and Portugal. The cry of freedom was loud and clear, and freedom of religion was one of its chief cornerstones. The opportunity for evangelical Christianity was plainly seen - one that had no parallel in Europe's history.

In that climate the EEC mushroomed in a few short years into a body of over a 100 workers serving in a dozen countries to the west of the Iron Curtain. Awareness of Europe's spiritual need was spreading among evangelical Christians on both sides of the Atlantic and financial support was matching every demand. Here was a modern mission-field whose population far outstripped that of Africa and the day had come for it to be evangelized. Besides EEC the new awareness brought an influx of missionaries into Europe and with them came not only various theological emphases, but sects and their heresies in abundance. It must also be remembered that doors in the traditional mission-fields were beginning to close and that missionaries were being diverted to the open countries of Europe in swelling numbers. And yet another feature which began thirty years ago and has intensified greatly since those days were the self-appointed, the free-lance and the short-term 'missionaries', most of them young people whose zeal and enthusiasm could be admired but whose qualifications and methods were at best inadequate. In effect, therefore, an influx of Christian societies and workers came to western Europe, some of them of sterling quality, while others left much to be desired. Freedom, apparently, is not always what it is made out to be.

If historic Catholicism and Protestantism were found wanting in post-war Europe, it cannot be said that evangelicalism fared a great deal better. The revivals James Stewart saw in the east were not repeated in the west, though there were many successful missions, in terms of attendances at meetings and the number of souls professing salvation. Yet these bore little resemblance to what had been known in former days. James was now leading a hundred or so missionaries, many of them godly and able; the work was bearing fruit in many countries and there were other agencies engaged in similar work. But for all the resources expended and all the good done, it had to be acknowledged that no deep and broad inroads were made into Europe's domains of false religion, ignorance and unbelief. The scene rather came to reproduce those prevailing in Britain and in America, with the same good points and the same weaknesses. This may be true of all missionary work but it was not what James Stewart had been looking and working for.

The annals of missionary enterprise are well stocked with accounts of sacrifice, the endeavours of a noble 'cloud of witnesses' extending from the early church to our own century. Some of the activities of evangelicals in post-war Europe will not find their way into those annals. What has been described as 'an irreligious solicitude for God and his cause' came to characterize too much of what was being done. It may have been what they had learnt at home, it could have been unguided zeal, it could also have been disappointment and frustration with the lack of ready success; but whatever the reason, views and methods more singular for novelty than biblical principles or spiritual power became widespread and, alas, were shared by a few in the ranks of EEC.

There were notable exceptions, of course, but the general situation gave rise to questions and misgivings which were not easily quelled. Concurrently, and surely inseparably from it all, the importance of local churches received only cursory notice, something that again caused dissatisfaction among members of the British branch of the EEC. That dissatisfaction was shared by James Stewart, certainly so far as evangelism was involved. Having proved God so remarkably in his own ministry, he had no time or patience with the brand of evangelism which became widespread in post-war years. He published several booklets on the subject, including *Hollywood Evangelism,* which emphasized the dangers of an evangelism which presented a 'popular Jesus', employed theatrical methods and resulted in many sham converts. 'In God's harvest field', he wrote that 'there has to be chaff among the wheat, but the tragedy is that today we often have more chaff than wheat.'

The stand he took over this issue cost him some friends, but it also helped to alert others to the whole question of worldly means being used for spiritual ends, not least those who had been brought into the work in Britain.

8. The parting of the ways

The rapid development of the European Evangelistic Crusade now took much of James Stewart's time and energy, but he still managed to spend periods in Europe pursuing the work which lay upon his heart - the work of evangelism, preaching and prayer for revival such as he had known in the eastern countries in pre-war days. He was now the president of an international missionary society and the innovator and inspiration of the work on the field. Combining the responsibilities of both roles was probably impossible and it was inevitable that he tended to leave others to shoulder the duties and decisions involved in administration.

Sad to relate, it was not long before the president was at odds with more than one national committee, chiefly because he found it difficult to operate within a framework of rules and regulations. James himself had been the prime mover in setting up that framework and it was essential if men and women of varying nationalities were to serve and co-operate effectively as one body of workers. But James could not see these rules as something within which he had to function, especially when leading groups of EEC missionaries in one place or another. James had of course been free as the wind in former days and had always done what he believed the Lord was leading him to do, however sudden or improbable that might appear to others. That was fine for him and nobody had any desire to curb him. On the contrary, some of us in the EEC wanted him to continue unhindered, believing that his was a ministry which is not given to many. But some semblance of order was necessary where the other workers were concerned, not so much to curb their activities as to ensure that everything was done 'decently and in order'.

The discords that arose were, however, no more than 'teething troubles' which would surely have been overcome with patience and goodwill. After all, the EEC as an organized society was young in years and experience and some problems of growth were to be expected. James Stewart was certainly anxious that his exceptional gifts and activities should not cause disquiet and tension, but nor did he want his own ministry to be stifled and accordingly he resigned his presidency and leadership of the EEC. Even so his affection for the mission remained undiminished and he continued to help it in every possible way, while the missionaries on the field and many in the home committees still looked to him for inspiration and leadership.

It was another issue which caused some disagreement in the middle 1950s, soon after each national section had been established and settled and the field work had been consolidated. When the EEC was formally constituted in the U.S.A. in 1944 the American section was designated the 'international headquarters'. This was no doubt done to provide a strong base for the future and was possibly in line with the practice of other societies in the U.S.A. Still there appears to have been some confusion, because a board of directors was not formed until 1947 so that for three years the international headquarters had only a council of reference.

In the meantime, the British issue of the *Voice of Europe*, the EEC quarterly magazine, announced in April 1946 that an international headquarters was to be located near London for easy links with the swelling number of missionaries and their labours on the nearby Continent. A house was purchased in St Leonards-on-Sea, Sussex, but no further reference was made to this nor to the American mission home in Buffalo, New York as the international headquarters, and neither the American Board of Directors nor the British equivalent was given international status or influence. Rather, they co-operated together and with other sections in Europe, through the Field Committee and the Superintendent, and the arrangement worked harmoniously and effectively and, so far as practical matters go, would most likely have lasted indefinitely.

However, the whole set-up came under strain when the

American Board announced itself and its office as being the international board and headquarters, a move which was rejected by all the other sections. The American section was larger than all the others put together and the financial support of the Field Superintendent and his office was borne entirely by the Americans, yet there were cogent arguments against having the international base of the EEC in Philadelphia, where the U.S. mission home and office had been moved. The U.S.A. is separated from Europe, not only by a vast ocean, but by an even wider cultural and economic gap. Further, each branch in Europe had been formed independently, with the British branch tracing its origin back to the late 1930s. Most important of all, a vigorous and growing gospel work in a dozen European countries could not, and should not, be controlled by a remote body of men, however good and godly, located over 3,000 miles away.

The American claim was countered by an alternative proposal for a truly international board to be formed, with representatives from every branch, and which could be entrusted with ultimate authority over the entire work including inter-branch relationships. James Stewart favoured this proposal but it foundered nevertheless on the American board's insistence on its own superior status and authority. While the argument was carried on by correspondence and discussion, it did not impinge upon any part of the actual EEC work and it should be said that the American brethren did not attempt to thrust their will upon the other sections and their work. On the contrary, they exercised wisdom and discretion and no real inter-branch problems arose at any time.

Be that as it may, in the latter part of 1957 a serious issue arose among members of the American branch and it is sadly ironic that a truly international board would have been able to intervene and resolve it. As it was, no authority existed in the EEC to deal with the problem and the consequences were disastrous to the American branch and distressing to many of its members, especially to James Stewart and his family.

There may have been other tensions within the U.S. branch but the eye of the storm which was soon to fragment it appeared elsewhere. During the hapless Hungarian uprising in the autumn of 1956, hordes of Hungarians fled for their lives to the west. The eastern border villages of Austria saw a veritable flood of refugees arriving every morning, their flight having been made under cover of night. The EEC, among others, provided substantial help and relief for the refugees, the resources being provided mainly by the American branch, through which large sums of money were raised for that purpose.

Much good work was done by EEC missionaries of the American branch but there were a few unwise actions, which need not be detailed now since they were, in any case, done in a crisis situation when feelings were stretched and the desire to help pitiful humanity was at a pitch. Besides, the situation was short-lived, as the uprising was quickly quelled by invading tanks and troops.

Some months later a full report of the events was received by the American Board, and this led to a very troubled situation among them, and ultimately to division. With the benefit of hindsight one feels that too much was made of the follies among the refugees, which were due to mistaken zeal rather than misconduct. It may well have been that other factors were involved and that what occurred in Austria in 1956 was just the straw that broke the camel's back.

The British and others offered help with mediation but this was rejected, and several appeals were made to the American friends to put their house in order. Finally a year's notice was given that the British branch would withdraw from the EEC if the U.S. section failed to resolve its difficulties, but all to no avail. At the end of that year the EEC disintegrated, with each branch going its own way.

Though he was not personally involved in the crisis, James Stewart could not have been a disinterested spectator; he had laboured long and hard to bring the mission into being and most of its missionaries had been called to the work through his ministry. He had also been personally involved in setting up the branches and, although he had withdrawn from the administration and routine matters of the mission, he had remained its inspirational leader and had continued to serve with its members in various countries.

But grievous though the blow must have been for him, James was not demoralized. His evangelistic and revival interest continued, in some sense on a wider scale, as he began to help missionaries in many parts of the world. To facilitate this he formed Gospel Projects and in due course his son-in-law Bob Doom became its director. He also wrote many books and booklets and these with other books were circulated freely among Christian workers throughout the world, the aim being to encourage them in evangelism and in prayer for a heaven-sent revival.

James Stewart's health was never robust and his tendency from his youth had been to push himself beyond the limits of his physical strength. As a result he occasionally suffered periods of ill health which necessitated rest, but in 1970 his condition deteriorated after a comparatively minor operation in an Edinburgh hospital. There followed four years of suffering which ended when the Lord took him in July 1975. He was sixty-five. Ruth Stewart later married a medical doctor in Czechoslovakia, an old friend from the days when she and James had worked there.

9. New beginnings

The British arm of the old EEC grew slowly but steadily in the later 1950s as young men and women from Britain took up service in several European countries. Though they still belonged to the international body of EEC missionaries, it soon became apparent to the British that close co-operation with their American counterparts in particular was not going to be easy, chiefly because of the substantial differences in their respective levels of financial support. The monthly allowance of the Americans was all but double that of the British, the reason being that the figures for both parties were based on the living standards of their home countries. British members were thus the poor relations in the EEC, and to avoid unwanted embarrassments they more often than not tended to work separately, though not entirely in isolation.

This may not be the time or place to discuss the subject in all its implications, but it can be said that the life-style of missionaries should always approximate to the moderate standards of the people among whom they minister rather than to those prevailing in their affluent home lands. This may mean an element of sacrifice, especially where the field countries are in the Third World. But the undesirability of missionaries living in a style which is far above that prevailing among the people to whom they preach and teach the gospel must surely be obvious to all concerned. Our Lord and his apostles certainly lived on the level of the common people, and so did all the great missionaries of yester-year.

Another important matter of finance separated the British workers from their American partners. The monthly allowances of the former were always subject to funds being available, while those of the latter were pledged by churches and friends in the U.S.A. The two sections were simply operating the systems commonly adopted in their respective countries. Hence, not only was the American allowance much higher than the British; it was also more reliable. The system adopted in Britain had long prevailed among missions and was usually thought to be consistent with 'living by faith'. In practice this meant that although a monthly allowance figure was fixed, it was always subject to the availability of adequate funds. Occasionally these were insufficient and the workers' monthly support suffered correspondingly. Admittedly, every such deficit was subsequently made good, but when the shortage occurred it created real difficulties.

The American friends experienced none of this because of their pledged support scheme, which meant that all candidates accepted for service in Europe were required to raise their own support *in toto* through regular gifts pledged by churches, groups and friends. It was only after the whole of their monthly needs had been promised that they took their departure for the field.

There were, and are, obvious advantages in such a scheme for the missionaries themselves and for the home-based staff, as all the burdens of finance are neatly packaged and taken care of. On the other hand there were also disadvantages, particularly when the scheme was rigidly operated. One American couple was accepted for service but languished at home for over two years while waiting for the required amount to be pledged.

Strangely enough, it was the way in which the American EEC enforced this system that led the British section to take a step which has had far-reaching benefits not foreseen at the time. Two American missionaries in Portugal were enabled to establish a church in a suburb of Lisbon and eventually one of the young men in the church felt the call to preach the gospel to his own Portuguese people. Poverty was rife in Portugal in those days and no financial help for the young preacher could be expected from the young church. The missionaries applied to their own board in America for help but this was declined on the ground that they had no funds other than those already designated for missionaries on the field. An appeal was then made to the British committee who, uninhibited by any inflexible scheme, decided to support the Portuguese national, subject of course, to available funds. In retrospect, this proved a crucial step for the British section (which was shortly to become the European Missionary Fellowship), the implications of which are still gathering strength and momentum. The young Portuguese became the forerunner of a still growing body of national workers who are now evangelizing and establishing churches in their own countries.

It was about this time too, in 1958, that the European Evangelistic Crusade began to break up. All attempts to resolve the problems besetting the American branch having failed, resignations followed among its members at home and in Europe. The Swiss branch also withdrew, together with the Field Committee and Superintendent, and there was really no course left for the British section other than to do the same and to constitute itself as an independent body with its own headquarters and organization. This was done in April 1959 and the title European Missionary Fellowship was adopted to express the principle of a group of workers sharing together in all things for the spread of the gospel in European countries.

The disintegration of the EEC was traumatic for all who had been involved in its vision and vigour, but the British section was not without some fortifying developments as it began its independent course. In the autumn of 1958 a conference of all the twenty-seven British missionaries, three national workers, home staff and committee members was held in Herne Bay, partly to foster our unity, as division was increasingly evident in the international EEC. This was a conference when it seemed the Lord himself drew near to bind us together for whatever lay ahead. Six months later when the independent European Missionary Fellowship was announced not one dissenting voice was raised among those affected by the decision.

By a merciful coincidence too, at the time of its emergence the EMF was able to move from its cramped premises at Tulse Hill in south-west London, to which it had moved in 1953, to a comparatively large house standing in its own grounds in Watford to the north-west of London. Besides providing useful accommodation for all immediate needs, the new headquarters and mission home had sufficient space to cater for further growth in years ahead. Thus within a year or so the new European Missionary Fellowship had been established and a fairly substantial base had been secured for all its practical needs.

The field situation was no less heartening. All EEC missionaries and their work had up till now been under the supervision of a single superintendent but this arrangement had collapsed with his resignation in 1958. From that time, British missionaries had liaised with the London office and this arrangement proved workable at least for the time being.

It was with profound thankfulness to God and to his supporting people in the U.K. that the newly formed mission was able to strengthen its stakes at home and to lengthen its cords in European fields as its workers laboured on in ten countries, from Norway in the north to Italy in the south and Portugal in the west.

While constituting the EMF was important enough, there were other developments at that time which in many ways were to prove even more significant. There was in particular a growing awareness in the work both abroad and at home in Britain, as if in tandem, that there were things to learn in our perceptions and matters to put into practice in the actual work in Europe.

With 100 men and women busily engaged in evangelism in a dozen countries it had gradually become apparent that some of their methods and activities owed more to human zeal and effort than to Bible standards and true spirituality. What was happening, of course, was that evangelistic modes and methods already prevalent in the western world were being introduced on the mission-field and EEC members were far from being the only people doing this. Many of EEC's personnel, however, had felt called to the work through James Stewart's ministry and he by spoken and written word was strongly opposed to such things. He had published books and booklets on the subject, at least one of which, *Hollywood Evangelism,* was widely commended. The tension between the principles they had been taught and practice on the field not unnaturally gave rise to a sense of unease among some of the missionaries.

The dissatisfaction with some of the field activities was paralleled and probably fuelled by a movement which was gathering momentum in Britain in the two decades following the war. Profound Christian truths which had been rediscovered and powerfully proclaimed by the Reformers and their successors, but which had been in comparative hibernation for long years, were being reasserted. The substance of those truths is that Christianity is essentially God-centred and that he is sovereign in salvation, as he is in every other realm. This fundamental doctrine and its implications for the work of the gospel in every sphere were gradually grasped within the ranks of the British EEC, and later the EMF, and the realization dawned that so much of modern evangelism and its methods were in fact the product of what was, and is, in reality a man-centred Christianity.

Another vital truth which gained renewed emphasis at that time was the place and function of the local church in evangelism, so much of which in those days, for EEC as for many other friends, was concerned with saving souls and not much more. A local church grounded upon the Word of God was seen to be the true end of evangelism and all else as unsatisfactory.

As these truths, and others, were understood and embraced, the necessity of separation from much that was still going on became clear. The process had already begun in the EEC days, and when EMF came into being the way was clear to implement the rediscovered doctrines and their practical outworking without undue hindrance. This was not done overnight, of course. Influence and persuasion were the means employed rather than pressure or criticism, and in the goodness of God the EMF grew in understanding, strength, numbers and, not least, in vision and concern to see the gospel of God's grace in Christ being sounded out in every part of Europe.

The restored significance of the local indigenous church was soon to cast fresh light upon the importance of native preachers and pastors. The decision to support one Portuguese worker had not been a matter of policy so much as a response to a special need. It was now seen to have been the first step in what was to be the express aim of future work. Not that hands were to be laid suddenly on any native aspirant for gospel service. It became rather a matter of prayer and expectation that God would use EMF missionaries already on the field to call and thrust forth men in the various countries to serve him among their own people and that EMF would be able to help those whom he so called.

This did not mean that British and other foreign missionaries would no longer be required. Foreign missionaries and foreign funds are as essential as ever to plant the Christian faith in countless pioneer situations, but when this is rightly done under the blessing of heaven, the message they preach must take root, grow and bring forth fruit - native fruit in souls saved and national pastors, evangelists, elders and deacons being appointed. In short, the full panoply of a New Testament church should always result from a New Testament missionary work. The Lord himself must be the Architect and Builder of such a church and any part his servants have in the work is their unspeakable privilege in being labourers together with him.

The ministry of foreign missionaries which goes on indefinitely under their leadership and control is in real danger of being regarded as a 'foreign import' by the local people and a barrier may be raised between preachers and hearers which is artificial and harmful. Where 'Christ is all' in reality, men and women of all classes and conditions will be saved and sooner or later some of them will be taken and put into the work of the ministry, and the Christianity which was brought from a distant land by foreign missionaries will become as native and indigenous to the local people as their own nationality, culture and tongue.

As the newly-formed EMF entered the 1960s the vision of establishing such gospel churches with their own national ministers grew clearer and stronger and it was not long before steps were being taken in obedience to that vision.

10. National workers

It is one thing to recognize that the goal of missionary endeavour must be the founding and building of local indigenous churches, but another to achieve it. EMF soon discovered that if such churches were to be planted, in southern Europe especially, the work of the missionaries would have to be supplemented in several ways. A combination of prolonged economic depression and traditional Roman Catholic influence meant that local funds were not readily available.

While the Common Market has brought real financial benefits to the southern Europeans it will take something more to overcome the effects of Roman Catholicism. Having no gospel of grace, the Catholic Church cannot inculcate the grace of giving; hence its development of 'means' to extract money from the 'faithful' - the sale of indulgences, candles and religious gadgets, masses for the dead etc. This in turn has over the centuries produced a mentality, the essence of which is to part with as little as possible for the church, and in any case there is usually hardly anything to spare in the oppressive poverty. Consequently converts from Catholicism do not become generous and sacrificial givers overnight. The grace of giving - that it is 'more blessed to give than to receive' - has to be learnt and where poverty prevails the lesson is difficult both to teach and to receive. Alas, many less deprived evangelicals in northern Europe have yet to emulate the Macedonian Christians of 2 Corinthians 8!

Up until the late 1970s young evangelical churches in southern Europe often included a number of widows, either converts or listeners, who were literally bereft of income. With no pensions and no social assistance they were dependent on their family, if there was one, or on charity. These women and others in similar circumstances inevitably became a charge on the offerings of several local groups of believers and EMF workers rightly accepted that time would be needed for these groups to become self-supporting.

One of the first needs of any new group of believers has invariably been for premises. A work begun in a home can soon outgrow the room available and eventually adequate premises will become essential. EMF has provided help for this need in many places by making interest-free loans which were repayable in ways acceptable to the local groups.

When native workers have been called to the work these have had to be supported in training and in their subsequent ministry. As their numbers have grown in EMF the cost entailed has often stretched the General Fund to the very limit.

Financial support is not, however, the chief difficulty where the development of indigenous churches with their own pastors is concerned. The inevitable cultural gap can also create problems which have to be resolved with patience and understanding. The differences between the cultures of northern Protestants and southern Catholics are marked and multifarious, affecting attitudes, standards and common customs. Where the differences impinge on biblical precepts and principles they are to be resolved through sustained Bible ministry and pastoral example and care, for the Word of God is one and the same for people of all cultures and climes. But where non-essential matters of local tradition are concerned allowances should be made lest any cultural gap be exacerbated unnecessarily. It is of no consequence that most evening services in Portugal, for example, begin at 9 p.m., that is, after the main meal of the day. None can object either that some young believers in Sicily often enjoy a *Spaghettati* - a communal meal of spaghetti - after the Sunday 5 p.m. service. Doubtless there are other, more peculiar cultural practices that could be mentioned, allowances for which may be more difficult to make, but they have to be made where no primary Bible truth is encroached.

It is in the realm of relationships that problems can often arise since the approach of southern Europeans can be much more casual than we in the north would like it to be. We like to be punctual, to keep arrangements and fulfil agreements - in short to be as good as our word. Our Latin friends would also claim to be as good as their word, but it might take a little more time because they are often more easily distracted! It is not a question of failure, still less is it perfidy; the clock and calendar are just not viewed in precisely the same way! This too is a cultural issue which has to be understood and coped with, even if this is not always easy.

Difficulties notwithstanding, the commissioning and support of national workers became the major part of EMF's activities over the two decades or so after its reformation in 1959. Men and some women of several countries applied for service in growing numbers and measures were first taken to provide them with Bible training and then to return them to serve among their own people. A course of Bible study was begun at the Watford headquarters in 1964, the aim being to ensure that all nationals who wished to serve with EMF were thoroughly grounded in biblical doctrines and were committed to biblical methods of communicating the gospel. Bible colleges were available in several countries, but some of their emphases in doctrine and methods were akin to those which EMF was in the process of forsaking.

Another important factor spurred on the plan to organize the training course at Watford, the value of which could not easily be quantified. The course was to be in English, which meant that all European nationals had to be taught the English language before commencing the main studies. This was seen as something of a chore and led a few prospective students to seek training elsewhere. But there were significant benefits to be won for the students themselves, for they gained access to the vast store of Christian literature in the English tongue, the like of which is not found in any other language. Most European countries had no Christian books of any significance until recent years and preachers and pastors were thus denied the help they need to fulfil their high calling. It has been a joy to see a succession of students returning to their own countries accompanied by crates of fine books which are now helping them to maintain a gospel ministry of some quality in their churches.

Another advantage was that, having once acquired English, students accepted into EMF were, and are, able to maintain regular communication not only with headquarters but with fellow-members in other countries as well by means of this common language.

By the late 1980s two-thirds of EMF's missionary body was made up of national workers - Greeks, Italians, French, Swiss, Spanish, Portuguese, Irish, as well as British and Americans and, latterly, a number of Polish churches and their pastors have become an essential part of the field. Though only a few of the pastors have had training, most have a knowledge of English.

It would be idle to pretend that the thirty years of progress thus briefly outlined have been free from those troubles which have always accompanied human affairs, including those of Christians. One of the crucial responsibilities in missions is the appointment of missionaries. Matters of call, qualifications and aptitude are obviously of paramount importance, but even when the utmost care is exercised in these and other realms, and even though many gifted and godly men share in the selection, training and commissioning of candidates, mistakes are still made and disappointments occur.

For example, one British missionary couple serving with the EMF, having evinced gifts of ministry and leadership on the field, became entangled with a sect that rejected the perfect sinlessness of Christ. They claimed that Christ's human body was the same as Adam's after the Fall and it was possible therefore for him to sin. But, they said, he had conquered the propensity to sin within him and had not become an actual sinner. He was, therefore, both an example and a help to the Christian to overcome indwelling sin. Strenuous efforts were made to show this couple that their new-found doctrine impugned the person of Christ and was in fact heretical, but all to no avail. With much sorrow the drastic step of dismissal had to be taken.

In later years a couple applying for service in Europe had to be rejected on doctrinal grounds. Both man and wife were highly qualified and worthy in all respects, but they had one serious chink in their armour: they did not accept the inerrancy of Scripture. In their view, the book of Jonah was not history, but rather a 'fine missionary tract', in which the actual story was a myth. Though they indicated that they would not propagate their view of Scripture, and in spite of their other excellent qualities their application had to be turned down with reluctance and regret.

It has, sadly, occasionally been necessary also to request the resignations of national workers; the problems caused great sorrow and are best not committed to writing. These were cases demanding firm decisions so that faith and practice were not compromised. They do not mean, however, that every EMF member crosses every 't' and dots every 'i' prescribed by a controlling body. What they do mean is that a standard of fundamental doctrines and their outworking in practice has to be upheld lest a drift sets in which will tend to lead the whole enterprise astray. Firm decisions and actions are sometimes painful and humility and charity are always desirable in those concerned.

There were other casualties also, understandable in most cases, but still unwelcome. The rigours of the climate in north Norway drove one British couple to withdraw to serve the Lord in Canada instead, while it caused serious health problems for two other couples who eventually had to leave the field. A fifth couple also found the conditions too harsh and gave up. One could only sympathize with these friends and feel thankful that those whose health was impaired have been fully restored.

To facilitate the expanding work on the Continent, an attempt was made in 1966 to set up a field office in eastern France and to appoint a field superintendent. The thinking behind the attempt was probably influenced by the existence of such an arrangement in the old EEC. But things did not work out satisfactorily and the task of supervising the field was transferred back to the Watford headquarters. In the event, this did not present too many difficulties since Britain is in Europe, now more than ever, and modern communications and transport made the travelling involved relatively easy. With hindsight, we can see too that having the headquarters and field office duties in one location has been a unifying factor as well as being an economical arrangement.

When it appeared that EMF was on an even course and many encouragements were giving cause for thankfulness and praise, the Executive Committee was faced with choosing a new chairman and one of its own number was proposed. The proposal met with opposition and a serious situation developed which threatened to do grave damage. Suffice it to say that the opposition held the view that the main body of EMF were people who testified to a call from God to serve him in the gospel, and whose work was chiefly concerned with preaching and caring pastorally for the souls of men and women. They believed therefore that the chairman of that body of necessity had to be a man similarly called to and experienced in the same work; in other words, a Christian minister. The person proposed was, however, a business man and, what made the situation even more difficult, he openly rejected the very notion of a call to the preaching office. The matter was finally resolved, with a minister appointed to the chair, but not before the proposed brother and the one proposing him felt obliged to resign. What was a very unhappy episode passed and while the outcome was satisfactory it was tinged with much regret, but it had forced everyone involved to think seriously of the issues raised.

Failures and disappointments notwithstanding, progress was made in several other areas during the 1960s. With the help of the Banner of Truth Trust books were published and circulated in France, an effort which was later carried on by Evangelical Press and others. EMF itself refrained from unduly diversifying its activities, its profound conviction being that the pre-eminent purpose to which it should devote itself was the preaching of God's truth for evangelism and church-planting. But, knowing the inestimable value of good Christian literature in countries where a famine has prevailed too long, it has pursued co-operation in literature work, especially with Evangelical Press, in France, Italy, Portugal and Spain.

By the end of the 1970s something had to be done with EMF's headquarters property in Watford, which in the meantime had become highly desirable for redevelopment. Local restrictions allowed only private residential use and it was decided to realize its considerable commercial value and to seek alternative premises. Quite unexpectedly EMF received an offer to rent Guessens in Welwyn, then owned by the Welwyn Evangelical Church, and this was gratefully accepted. The move was made in 1981. Guessens is a fine old country house in the lovely village which was once a staging post on the Great North Road, just twenty-five miles from Marble Arch in the centre of London. The house is now owned by EMF and, besides staff and missionary accommodation, caters for office needs and those of the School of Evangelism.

11. Europe is a mission-field

That James Stewart should venture forth in 1935 as a missionary to Europe can only be understood as the result of the call and guidance of God. Evangelical missions of those days were almost entirely preoccupied with those dark and primitive sub-continents we now describe as the Third World. The modern missionary movement had begun in those regions as a 'mission to the heathen', that is, the people of the world among whom the name of Jesus had not been heard. And where it had begun, so it had largely continued for a century and a half, with precious little thought given to the masses living within the sphere known as Christendom. Thus it was that in the first half of the twentieth century for most evangelical Christians the world's mission-fields were located in Africa, India, the Far East and South America. It was in those places that countless people were living in total ignorance of God and Jesus Christ and wholly bereft of the blessings of the Christian faith so richly enjoyed in more favoured shores.

Scottish evangelicals before World War II would certainly have shared this outlook, understandably, seeing that their missionary annals included such giants as William Burns, David Livingstone, John Paton and Mary Slessor. It was therefore the more surprising that James Stewart, as a very young man and wholly independent of the strong influences around him, should be constrained to go to Europe. The only adequate explanation is that God called him to a people whose great spiritual need was not even recognized at the time. Enoch Wangberg and Oswald Blumit were instruments in God's providence to open James' eyes, but these two young men had contact with a number of other British believers who apparently were not greatly moved by their reports. The fact is that a partial blindness regarding the true nature of missions had descended upon many Christians in the west, one that strangely persists in some measure even in our time.

In reaching out to the heathen who had not heard the name of Jesus, missionaries had immediately been faced with their pathetic social conditions, involving not only ignorance but deep suffering resulting from disease, famine and gross superstition. With the love of Christ in their hearts they had to do something to relieve the distress of the people they had come to evangelize and almost inevitably social relief became a part of gospel missions, and rightly so. The great Spurgeon summed this up in his own inimitable way: 'If you are giving a tract to a starving man', he said, 'wrap it in a sandwich!'

But while it was entirely right and proper for Christian missions to take medical and educational activities on board, with the passing years certain pitfalls developed into which not a few have fallen. Numerous missionaries found the demands of social relief crowding out the work of saving souls. Others of weak evangelical convictions remained content to toil sacrificially in the social realm, almost to the total neglect of evangelism. Hence, one way and another, for many Christians, missions became inseparable from programmes for the physical, mental and social well-being of the backward and deprived multitudes of the Third World. Now, with the widespread adoption of liberation theology even by professing evangelicals, the departure from taking the saving gospel to 'heathen who have never heard the name of Jesus' is far advanced and missions are not what they once were.

Yet another consequence of the social conditions factor in the traditional mission-fields is of significance for us as we think of Europe. Because well-nigh all missionary endeavour for over a century had been confined to Third World countries, the deprived social conditions prevalent in those countries became identified for many Christians with their spiritual need and eventually were accepted as being an essential ingredient in the popular understanding of a mission-field. The common assumption seemed to be that

Christian missions were intended as much to alleviate human misery in the present world as to save souls for eternity.

So, with the general opinion running so strongly to far distant and primitive regions of the world, who would stop and look at Europe? Why should they anyway? Christianity had thrived in Europe. If Palestine had been its cradle and where it had been weaned and learnt to walk, it was in Europe that it grew up and became strong. Those very benefits of Christianity that missions were taking to relieve the misery of the world's backward peoples were widely enjoyed by Europeans. The world's oldest hospitals, universities and schools were in Europe, while economic and material benefits unimagined in other continents were a commonplace aspect of life. Behind it all, of course, were the historic expressions of the Christian religion, Roman Catholicism, the Eastern and Greek Orthodox Churches and Protestantism, which together encompassed the whole of Europe leaving few if any of its people uninfluenced in some degree. Small wonder really that the prevailing missionary outlook did not take Europe into its reckoning.

But its Christian history and superior social conditions notwithstanding, viewed from a faithful biblical standpoint, Europe was, and still is, a vast mission-field. Though Scripture has much to say about the poor and leaves none who believe it free to ignore them, its overriding concern is for the lost souls of men and women. Jesus Christ came to preach the gospel to the poor, not merely to relieve their physical distress. He had eternity in view, and the liberation he died to secure for mankind was not from man's social afflictions, but rather from the chains of sin and the tyranny of Satan. Alone in heaven and earth,

He breaks the power of cancelled sin
And sets the prisoner free.

In other words, the unique message of true Christianity is spiritual, having to do with people of all kinds and categories who are lost in sin. It views men and women, whatever their physical conditions, not in comparison with others in better or worse conditions, but as in the sight of God. And in his all-seeing eye there is no difference between the cultured, prosperous Westerner and the starving, semi-naked jungle-dweller. 'All have sinned and come short of the glory of God.'

When this incontrovertible biblical truth is received and its solemn implications are accepted, civilized Europe and its masses take on a new light. Although they have been 'Christianized' in varying ways and means they are, alas, generally still unevangelized. With all the advantages of a Christian influence, with its theism, ethics and morality, the many and mixed millions have yet to hear in some faithful way the gospel as it is in Jesus. Education has greatly helped, prosperity has made the vast majority comparatively comfortable in homes and health, and it would be difficult to find any whose bodies are emaciated through famine. The benefits, to be sure, are many and ample, so much so that all should be well in Europe. But whence came the two world wars and why are violence, robbery, murder, dishonesty, immorality, and so on at such a pitch in modern Europe, stretching from east to west and missing few in between? The reality is clear: while material blessings have multiplied and spread in our supposedly Christianized continent, its people still are largely destitute of that salvation which is in Christ by faith alone.

Historic Christianity in Europe has in general been unbiblical, with the result that its multitudes are still lost sinners and thus are in no way different from the Third World masses. Europe is, and has been for long centuries, as real a mission-field as any part of heathendom, because a mission-field has to do with men and women who do not know Christ and his saving grace. Where they are found and in what temporal condition is not all that relevant except in secondary matters of approach and method of reaching them with the gospel.

There can be no doubt that while the British evangelical constituency of the early twentieth century was almost wholly preoccupied with far-flung missionary realms, James Stewart had his eyes opened to recognize the immense and urgent need of the nations so near at hand, and God then summoned him to become one of the very few who were labouring to meet that need. We know that he obeyed that summons with his trust in God to guide and to provide for him. But was he also aware that not many Christians at home would readily share his vision? This could well have been so.

What the young Scots evangelist found in this latter-day

mission-field could scarcely be computed or accurately described. A form of Christianity held the millions captive in most nations, while the faith of the Bible was declining in those areas where it was not actually being suppressed or its adherents persecuted. There was indeed a true remnant in many countries and some of them were actively preaching Christ and winning souls. James Stewart found warm acceptance among them, but they were small in numbers and were often overwhelmed by official Christendom which held the multitudes in thrall. Pre-war Roman Catholicism still held sway in most European countries and, besides holding its 'faithful' people in utter ignorance of evangelical religion, it was also able to proscribe all who sought to preach it. An almost identical situation obtained in eastern Europe where the Orthodox Church was in control except where Communism was striving to banish it.

There are professing Christians who accept the Roman Catholic and Orthodox Churches as validly Christian, but if Christianity is pre-eminently a matter of sinners being saved by grace through faith in Jesus Christ and his atoning death, these churches are certainly not Christian. It is true that they profess belief in the Trinity, the Bible, the miracles and in the death of Christ for sinners at least in some sense, and if these truths alone comprise essential Christianity, then they are Christian. But what about the gospel of salvation? Does this not lie at the very heart of biblical revelation? Cast a brief glance at what Roman Catholicism teaches about salvation, though claiming to believe that Christ died to save sinners. The church, with the pope at its head, is central in Rome's salvation tenets, which say that there is no salvation for anyone outside that church. And Rome has systematized its way of bestowing salvation. First baptismal regeneration, then confirmation, followed by auricular confession of sin, penance, priestly absolution, the mass, extreme unction, purgatory - they claim that all these are necessary to salvation and vast throngs throughout the centuries have believed and practised them, and yet more do so still. The Orthodox churches hold many of these doctrines in common with Rome.

That all this can be said to be Christian is surely fallacious beyond measure. It is rather man-made religion with some cardinal biblical truths overlaid by human superstitions, far removed from the faith of the gospel. Whatever exceptions there may have been

Europe, approximately 20% of the world's population - a mission-field in our backyard.

and still are, the tragic people beholden to this false religion need to hear the truth. They are to be seen as a mission-field with an urgent need to hear the free offer of the gospel of Christ. It was to these people that James Stewart was sent and, as well as himself being used of God for the salvation of a host of lost sinners, he became the forerunner of a growing body of missionaries engaged in the same divine calling. The spiritual need of Europe persists, hardly diminished, even if it is more widely recognized fifty years beyond the 1930s. Its people are said to comprise twenty per cent of the world's population, which means nearly a billion men, women and children, the great majority of whom are still without the true knowledge of God in Christ and have none to tell them.

It is undoubtedly safe to assume that western Europe alone has more people who have never heard the true gospel of salvation than the entire population of Africa. In unambiguous terms they must be regarded as unevangelized, whatever some people may claim. To all intents and purposes the great missionary movement initiated by William Carey and others concentrated its resources and labours on the heathen in remoter climes and bypassed the advantaged 'heathen' in their own backyard, as it were. This is not at all to suggest that it was wrong to send missionaries to distant lands; rather, it is a question of 'this ought ye to have done and not left the other undone'. The command is to 'preach the gospel to every creature', including our own local equivalent of Jerusalem, Judea and Samaria as well as the 'uttermost part of the earth'. The harsh reality is that, despite its historical advances and its current cultural and religious structures, Europe is a mission-field of immense proportions - the cry of the man of Macedonia has not become irrelevant.

12. In retrospect

Following the Reformation in the sixteenth century, religious Europe was eventually divided into three main sections which, in general terms, persisted until the twentieth century was well on its way. In the meantime there were shifts and changes in the political play of many countries, but intrigues, revolutions and wars did not materially alter the major structures of European Christendom for more than three centuries because almost invariably politics and religion were in league with the latter, calling the tune.

The three broad divisions were the east, which was dominated by the Orthodox Church, the south, where the Roman Catholic Church held almost total sway, and the north, where Protestantism was firmly established in most of the principal countries. Though the respective powers were mutually exclusive, there was considerable overlapping, but neither these nor various significant developments materially affected the established pattern and its prevailing powers. The violent French Revolution of the late eighteenth century, for example, was powerfully influenced by rationalism but Roman Catholicism remained the official religion of France though wounded and scarred in the aftermath.

From the sixteenth century onwards repeated attempts were made to restore Britain to the papal embrace, but these were variously thwarted, while a succession of events like the Puritan revival, Cromwell's Commonwealth, the Glorious Revolution of 1688 and the Evangelical Awakening nearly a century later ensured that reformed Christianity would continue in Britain for generations to come.

Thus for around three centuries, minor variations apart, the scene in Europe continued virtually unchanged. During the nineteenth century, however, unseen forces were developing which, in combination with political ambition and military adventure, were in the twentieth century to change the face of Europe and affect the whole world.

With the Great War of 1914-18, Communism came to Russia and the old order was destroyed almost overnight. The Orthodox Church suffered a blow but staved off extinction partly through deft diplomacy and compromise. Even so its domination was broken, perhaps beyond recovery. How Russian evangelicals, small and scattered in the main, have held on through privations and persecutions is a story not yet fully told; but they have indeed held on.

What took root in Russia in 1917 was widely extended through the Second World War and the Iron Curtain which ensued. Atheistic Communism took over the whole of Eastern Europe, vowing to snuff out religion of any kind. It failed, of course, as successive reports have increasingly demonstrated. Least of all could evangelical Christianity be suffocated as believers in other eastern countries joined those in Russia to withstand and repulse the onslaught of atheism. News of them brought joy and sorrow to evangelicals in the west: sorrow because of the suffering of many believers in cruel prison camps, and joy as their perseverance shone brightly in a dark world and maintained the faith the enemy sought to destroy.

It is no reflection on these believers and their faithfulness to call in question the content and tone of some of the reports and appeals on their behalf which circulated in Britain and all points west. So often prayer was urged for those persecuted saints as if they were in danger of capitulating to their tormentors and evangelical Christianity itself was about to be extinguished among them. It may not have been intended to give this impression but this was certainly the effect produced by some of the material published which, even if basically true, was manipulated for propaganda purposes.

The fact was, of course, that true Christianity was, and still is, safer with the persecuted believers of the east than with their easygoing counterparts in the west. It has always been safe in the hands of those who have little and suffer a lot, but is it safe among those who have so much and endure so little, if at all? If biblical Christianity is in any danger in this latter part of the twentieth century it is probably in the west, where the pursuit of comfort and pleasure is no less obvious among those who profess faith than those who profess little or nothing, and where compromise is the order of the day. Persecution of any kind is always grievous, but it does concentrate mind and heart on the things the true Christian cannot surrender.

In tow with the implied suggestions that the faith was endangered in the east was the wide use of emotive terms like the 'Underground Church' - the insinuation being that believers behind the Iron Curtain were operating in strict secrecy, rather like the underground forces in France and Holland during the last war. This may have had powerful appeal in the West but could it have been really true? Certainly Christians facing persecution have often gone underground in some senses, hence the catacombs, caves and lonely meeting places of church history. Yet, by its very nature true Christianity cannot remain secret for long in any situation. Believers meeting clandestinely because of fierce opposition is one thing, but they have to be believers in their homes and places of work and in society generally, and their faith and discipleship have to be made known. Thus it has been in the east.

In any case, the 'underground' notion has been resented by many eastern believers whose profession of faith has been unequivocally above-ground, even in the face of opposition and trouble. This is why so many of them have languished in prison camps and suffered in many other ways; refusing to cower, they professed and practised their faith in every essential way. One pastor in the east was asked by a visitor from the west: 'What about the underground church?' 'There is no such thing here,' was the sharp reply.

While it is not only evangelicals who have suffered under Communism, it is they who appear to have been in the most trouble, the reason being surely that their belief of the truth is not easily shaken or compromised. It is true certainly that Communism has had to make concessions to Orthodox, Roman and Protestant churches where these have been numerically very strong. The notable example, though not the only one, is Poland, where Roman

Catholicism has survived two generations of militant Communism and, with the incentive of a Polish pope, has emerged possibly stronger than ever. The long-running issue of the illegal trade union Solidarity has never failed to capture the headlines of the west; what has not been apparent is that in reality it is a clash between Communism and Catholicism. Solidarity, according to Polish evangelicals, is conceived and influenced by the priests, and many believers have not supported it for that reason.

None of the religious powers has fared too well in other countries of eastern Europe, but none has been routed either. Not enough is known about the detailed situation in those countries for informed comment, but it is general knowledge that religious activity in every country behind the Iron Curtain has been severely curtailed but not entirely extinguished. Now that *glasnost* has arrived there will be a resurgence of all the historic churches, not least, we can be sure, of evangelical Christianity. It could also be that these countries, closed for half a century and largely overlooked before that, will become new mission-fields for those in the west who cherish Protestant and reformed Christianity.

The situation in southern Europe over the same period has been dominated by the Roman Catholic Church. Its position and power were certainly breached by the Reformation, but the Counter-Reformation and the infamous Inquisition turned back the tides of reform and revival, notably in Italy and Spain, and in other parts as well. Spain's connections with Holland in the sixteenth century meant that Catholic Spaniards, able to travel to Holland, came into close contact with the Dutch Reformation and many of them were converted and took the new faith back with them to Spain. These were rich upper-class people who had the time and means to travel. Returning to Spain, they restricted their witnessing to people of their own class, many of whom embraced the new-found faith. When the ferocious Counter-Reformation got under way it did not have to cope with a great movement involving the common people, for very few of them had been reached with the gospel. It was among the upper classes that the 'infection' had spread and it was they, comparatively only few in number, who were burned in the outrageous *autos-da-fe* as Roman Catholicism reasserted itself. What a tragedy for Spain!

In Italy too the fires of Reformation were quenched by a ruthless power which was fighting for its very existence. There were many such fires to put out too! The story of Peter Martyr alone puts this beyond doubt. As a monk in Naples he embraced justification by faith and with others began to preach it with marked success. Before 1540 an evangelical church was established in Naples which numbered titled and other eminent people in its ranks. Martyr was moved to Lucca near Pisa, where again he preached so powerfully that Lucca was soon reckoned to have more reformed Christians than any place in Italy. The inmates of the convent where Martyr was prior were said to be *in toto* converted to faith in Christ alone and a large monastery south of Pisa was similarly affected, not one monk excepted. By 1543 Pisa too had an evangelical church, as did many other centres throughout the country. Here again the Inquisition, resolute and pitiless, laid waste the churches which had sprung to life and their preachers and members were scattered or flung into dungeons to be tortured into submission or die.

In the period 1545-1563, the Council of Trent sealed the Counter-Reformation, not only reaffirming the established dogmas of Rome, but actually strengthening them, and these, for three centuries to come, were to keep southern Europe behind an 'Iron Curtain' of Rome's making. Closed frontiers and persecution kept evangelical religion in the various countries at bay but failed to destroy it within, and Catholicism reigned without serious challenge in every major realm of life throughout most areas of southern Europe.

It was after the twentieth century was almost half gone that cracks appeared in Rome's monolithic structure, but the causes had been fermenting for several years past, one interacting with another to produce a dramatic change in lands which had languished so long under papal domination. Space will only permit us to list a few of those causes and note briefly some of their impact in the southern countries. Modern communications have no doubt played a key part in the process, their effect being to open up and to draw these countries into the highway along which western nations were moving with quickening pace. Economic prosperity once seen and envied from afar became something to be shared; education and politics were opened likewise to views and practices which were commonplace elsewhere. Perhaps most significant of all, tourism gathered momentum, bringing much-needed foreign currency to poor nations and, inevitably, compelling people of the Catholic south to have close dealings with those of the Protestant north.

The cumulative effect of all this can hardly be exaggerated, and particularly in the sphere of religion. Roman Catholicism is still the most powerful single influence in the south of Europe but its once tenacious hold on men and women is now little more than nominal for large numbers of them. Its massive churches are often empty and its institutions are in decline. In Italy, for example, many parishes are without priests, while many of the priests available are not native Italians. Much has been made of Pope John XXIII's openness towards non-Catholics and of the relaxing tendencies of Vatican Council II as indicating a change of attitude in Catholicism. The truth is that Rome's medieval stance had to go, not because of any change of heart or dogma; rather, because of the facts of life, something had to be done to halt the slide!

The huge monastery south of Pisa where Peter Martyr preached and every monk once professed faith in Christ alone was found by the present writer in 1962 to be occupied by only two monks. When asked the reason for this state of affairs, one of the monks said, 'We have a crisis on our hands in the church!' That 'crisis' was the rapid reduction in the 'faithful', waning political influence and growing economic stringency. Something had to be done, and so the changes followed, but there was no real change as the eventual appointment of Pope John Paul II and the subsequent course of action adopted by him have shown only too clearly.

As the power of Rome has ebbed, the countries of southern Europe have been unlocked for evangelical Christianity. With the advent of Mussolini and his notorious concordat with the Vatican, evangelism in Italy was stifled and some who professed it were persecuted, including native believers. EMF workers in Sicily minister to a small group of believers in Lucca Sicula, a meeting which began in the simple home of a widow whose husband died in prison over fifty years ago. He was an evangelical stalwart who refused to yield to the persecution to which that concordat gave birth. Others suffered like him. Foreign missionaries were refused residence permits and Italy was closed to the outside evangelical world. The same thing was true of Spain and Portugal, and in lesser measure of some other countries - such was the vice-like grip in which they were held by a totalitarian Roman Catholicism.

By the late 1960s and early 1970s, however, the situation in each country was transformed, chiefly for the reasons sketchily outlined above. It was in 1967 that a new law was pushed through the Spanish *Cortez* (parliament) to enforce a freedom of religion which previously had been a mere theory. The argument used on that occasion was the annual influx of tourists from Protestant northern Europe and the great wealth they were bringing to Spain. They were finding many Protestant buildings closed and sealed by the police. If the tourists were to be encouraged they had to be free to worship as they desired. In the face of this argument and its vital economic undertones, not even the Catholic hierarchy and its agents could hold out.

What this new situation in Latin Europe has meant is that an opportunity to preach and teach biblical Christianity exists, the like of which has not been known hitherto. Suffice it now to say that nothing should be allowed to hinder this opportunity being seized and used to the full.

Strange as it may seem, the fading sway of Catholicism in southern Europe has been matched by the tragic decline of Protestantism in the north. The faith of the Reformers and their successors captured the northern part of Germany, Holland, the whole of Scandinavia, Britain and parts of France and Switzerland. Through the English language it reached out to North America and Australasia and eventually was carried by a noble band of missionaries to all points of the compass.

In the meantime, while southern nations languished under false religion, those of the north felt the impact of Bible truth and ethics. Freedom and education spread, morality and motivation increased and, all in all, an ever-improving standard of life, especially among the hitherto unprivileged masses, became commonplace throughout the northern countries. Those undoubted benefits remain, but the spiritual force which brought them about has been decaying during the greater part of the twentieth century.

Detailed analysis of the causes is beyond our present purpose; many are advanced which are secondary and in some instances are effects rather than causes. The real cause, I firmly believe, lies in the rejection of the Bible as the sole authority of faith and practice, which is of the essence of Protestantism. The early nineteenth century saw the rise of rationalistic attitudes towards the Bible and its supernaturalism; higher criticism developed and liberalism became fashionable, notably in the theological faculties and in the pulpits of reformed Europe. The supreme authority of the Bible was discarded, to be followed inevitably by the loss of its pre-eminent message of salvation by grace through faith. Things continued in the Protestant churches as before: the Bible was still read and parts of it preached, the same hymns were sung and prayers made. To all intents and purposes nothing had changed but, in fact, apostolic Christianity, which had been rediscovered and restored through the Reformation, had been abandoned and the consequences began to make themselves known. Within a hundred years, churches and their denominations which had been strong and seemingly unshakeable were crumbling. Various explanations were advanced - two world wars in particular, the age of science, the pursuit of pleasure, and others, all of which have some relevance. The primary cause remains, namely a pseudo-Christianity whose gospel is shorn of the supernatural elements of God's Word.

By the mid-twentieth century Protestantism was in such decline that strong measures were called for and Ecumenism was born. The diagnosis of Protestant decay was its denominational divisions; unity was seen as the only hope, including unity with the Roman church which, if anything is now more truly papal and heretical than it was in pre-Reformation days (the dogmas promulgated by the Council of Trent, papal infallibility and Mariolatry, for example, are all later additions).

There is a certain logic in this, in that there is no real reason why those whose religion is not securely anchored to Scripture, and is therefore open to human views and influences, should not join Rome. Birds of a feather can and do flock together! It would be an advantage surely if all extra-Scripture professing Christians were lumped together under one umbrella, papal or not, because the difference of faith and doctrine too long blurred and compromised would at last be plain for all to see! Authentic evangelicals could then with meaning quote Joshua of old: 'As for me and my house we will serve the Lord.'

Whatever the future holds in that respect or any other, the stark present reality is that Protestant northern Europe has become a vast latter-day mission field. While it continues to thrive in most temporal realms, spiritually and morally it is like the dog which returned to its own vomit. The capitals of reformation have become the centres of every conceivable vice and sin, natural and unnatural. Hedonism is unrestrained while the true knowledge of God and of the gospel of Christ fades into mists of ignorance and superstition.

If a mighty reformation was needed in the sixteenth century, how much more is it needed in this late twentieth century!

13.
Modern Europe

While its post-Reformation history is obviously significant in any understanding of modern Europe, more recent movements, political, ethnic and economic, are bringing new and critical influences to bear upon its current situation. Some of these are likely to figure prominently for good or ill in any strategy for future gospel work and, for that reason, must at least be noted in this brief review.

The European Economic Community (EEC), for example, has become a prominent fact of life in western Europe as each of its member countries reaps its burgeoning material benefits. These in turn are viewed with envy by a small queue of would-be members who are applying to join, including Turkey, whose Europeanism is perhaps more sanguinary than real. Economic prosperity apart, substantial benefit in other realms has accrued from the EEC and its growing power. Most important of all for Europe and the world in the temporal sense is the era of peace which it has undoubtedly fostered. The two world wars of the twentieth century broke out among the very nations which are now united in the EEC, and one has only to visit the heart-rending cemeteries of France, Holland and Germany to gain some appreciation of the appalling cost in young lives of those wars and to feel thankful that nations which devastated each other not so long ago are now working together for peace and mutual prosperity.

It is gratifying also that political stability and liberalization have resulted in one or two EEC countries where dictatorships and oppression once prevailed. Evangelicals in particular are happy that EEC membership has swept away restrictions which formerly militated strongly against evangelistic activities in Catholic-dominated countries whose doors were closed to foreign missionaries. It will be interesting in this connection to see what will happen in Moslem Turkey if and when its application for EEC membership is successful!

Whatever the future may hold in this respect, the EEC has brought freedom to countries where it had conspicuously been in short supply, especially in the realm of religion, which is our chief interest here. When Britain was about to join the Common Market in 1973 many fears were expressed that, among other things, membership would bring it once again under the malign spell of the Roman Catholic Church. Events have proved otherwise thus far but, while Catholicism in reality remains what it always has been, there can be no guarantee that it will not, one way or another, succeed in re-establishing its all-pervasive influence. It will most certainly try by every trick in the trade.

What the EEC has achieved in the political sphere is matched by its economic success. Western Europe today is extremely rich and confidently expected to become even more so as the last obstacles to free trade, travel and employment are abolished in 1992. Greater prosperity for all countries in the EEC is forecast which, if realized, will make almost the whole of western Europe into a consumer's paradise and concurrently an ever-expanding playground for its materialistic and well-heeled people.

It would seem too that the prosperity of the west has stirred the Communist empire in the east to reconsider their ways. Their empty shelves and shortages have long depressed a people who, in spite of the Berlin Wall and other restrictions, have caught glimpses of the overflowing abundance among their western neighbours. If this is what *perestroika* really means, we may yet see Russia and its allies abandoning their stale and failed economic policies in favour of those which have proved so successful in Western Europe. And if this is achieved, Europe east and west will become a vast materialist continent, with its multitudes enjoying the 'good life', hopefully in perpetuity.

What this really amounts to is that for modern European man his life will increasingly 'consist in the things he possesses'. The pursuit of money and what it secures in the pursuit of pleasures of every kind will become the be-all and end-all of life. Mammon will be god and religion of any kind will only be a form of insurance, if not entirely irrelevant and unwanted.

With efficient birth control preventing new life and medical expertise prolonging old life, it is thought that Christendom in some form will retain its ageing adherents and even become proportionately stronger as the younger population declines numerically. At best, however, this would be of only short duration and the religion itself in any case would be largely nominal. The real prospect is that western Europe will become a religious and moral wasteland in which greed and sexual sins will thrive, with all the consequences they entail.

Pope John Paul II is said to be deeply concerned about this prospect and anxious to do something about it. Addressing the European Parliament, he spoke of the danger of God being excluded from Europe's projects. He is said to be anxious to lead Europeans to look once again to their religious roots and, since over two-thirds of them have been baptized into the Roman church, this can mean only one thing. What needs to be seen and accepted by all who are Bible-believing Christians is that the conservative John Paul has a two-fold ministry: one is to guard against any real change in Catholicism - hence his appointment of conservative bishops in several countries - and the other is to recover the ground the Catholic Church has lost in most European countries. Those who know that totalitarian Catholicism was decisively breached by the faith of the Reformation will also know that the only sure resistance to a resurgence of it is the active propagation of the same reformed faith and its gospel of salvation. This, too, is surely the only safe and satisfactory answer for Europe's growing moral and spiritual vacuum.

Of parallel significance with papal hopes and plans for Europe is the developing role of Ecumenism. Despite the ordination of women and multi-faiths trends, unity with Rome is still its ultimate goal and the portents suggest that this will be achieved because the erstwhile Protestant denominations and their leaders, including, alas, some professing evangelicals, have finally come to accept Roman Catholicism as validly Christian.

While this may cause regret, there can hardly be real surprise because there is a logical inevitability in it. When the supreme and final authority of the Bible is abandoned and its divine doctrines are lost, there is really no compelling reason why anyone should stand apart from the Roman church. Where the supremacy and divine authority of Scripture are lost and the doctrines of grace are rejected, the Catholic system has a lot to offer in papal authority, tradition, ritualism and sacramentalism for the unregenerate who want religion and morality of some kind as means to save themselves. That it is all a form of godliness which denies its power they cannot know, and with blind leaders and blind people the end can only be a ditch of superstition and darkness.

Assuming that Ecumenism will circumvent and overcome the various obstacles and achieve its aim of a world church, the reactions of Bible believers will be mixed and perhaps conflicting. There could be a real advantage for them in having to cope with a so-called 'united church' which is popularly accepted throughout the world as the standard-bearer of Christianity. At least the confusion of many years will be dispelled and the essential difference between reformed and unreformed Christianity will become more starkly apparent. To be sure, biblical evangelicals will be a small minority, under pressure and subject to criticism of varying kind and degree, but compared with the disarrayed mishmash of this century and its harmful effects, this would surely be a real benefit. Spurgeon once noted that seamen preferred a storm to a fog!

What could spell trouble for all concerned with evangelism and the conversion of sinners would be a prohibition on proselytizing which a world church might well try to impose. The argument would be that since it is the accepted custodian of Christianity, to allow other versions of it to spread would only cause fresh divisions. The emphasis on human rights and the freedom of the individual may be strong enough at present and in the foreseeable future to prevent such a development, but the influence of a world church in political and governmental circles could be subtle and persuasive enough to bring about changes.

Lest anyone should think this possibility to be remote and over fanciful it should be noted that the prohibition of proselytizing is already common in Arab and other nations, and is not unknown in Israel also. Both Jews and Arabs, among others, demand freedom for themselves in non-Jewish and non-Arab countries, while

Mosque in Berea, Greece

denying it to Christians in their own. This may not be all that significant where Israel is concerned, seeing that Judaism is not missionary-minded. But Islam is aggressively bent on spreading itself world-wide, and it has all the resources needed for the task. Oil-riches are seemingly unlimited and are currently being devoted to building mosques, schools and colleges in ever-growing measure.

The ground forces which are financed and equipped for this Islamic advance are the immigrants and their families in large and still growing numbers who, since the mid-twentieth century, have settled in several European countries and in a remarkably short time have established a virile Moslem presence in each one. They already constitute a serious challenge to western societies, their cultures and traditions, and especially to Christians who still cherish a missionary vision and zeal. That vision must embrace the opportunities for evangelism which the influx of Moslems obviously presents to evangelicals in Britain.

While Sikhs and Hindus, together with the modern sects, are not to be ignored either, it is the threat of militant Islam which looms large for Europe in the near future. What has been described as a 'human time-bomb' is gathering strength and impetus in the population explosion in Arab nations adjacent to Europe. Greece's 10,000,000 is already overshadowed by Turkey's 50,000,000, but while the former is expected to remain static for the next quarter century, the latter is estimated to reach 100,000,000. Moreover, a recent United Nations report shows that in 1950 two-thirds of the Mediterranean populations were Europeans belonging to countries stretching from Gibraltar to the Bosphorous. By the year 2025, says the report, the situation will be reversed, with only one-third being of European nationality, and the Mediterranean will have become an Islamic and mainly Arab sea.

Whatever the political and economic implications of such a transformation may be, those in the religious sphere will be very far-reaching, not only for the countries in the Mediterranean basin, but throughout Europe too. Not only is Islam confidently aggressive, with fanatical elements and unlimited resources among the swelling numbers of immigrants already living in the major European nations; it has what amounts to a fifth column which is busily engaged in preparing the ground for what could be another Moslem invasion of Europe. The first one, in the seventh and eighth centuries, was made by force of arms and foundered in A.D. 732 in France and was eventually repulsed. The new invasion is more subtle and insidious, but none the less real, and something other than carnal weapons will be required to resist and conquer it.

Assuming this picture of Europe as it approaches and enters the twenty-first century is only realized in part, the future for true Christianity and all who profess and practise it will be troubled and demanding. With sinful humanity in the grip of materialism or held in thrall by one false religion or another, the cause of the gospel of God will be under siege, spiritually certainly, and possibly physically too. We in the west are so attuned to a situation where freedom of religion is an inalienable right that we suppose it always will be so. We cannot easily conceive it otherwise but how wrong we could be! There are many nations in our modern world where freedom of religion is denied and where Christianity in particular is opposed with violence. What is more, the number of such nations is actually growing, even in this 'enlightened' twentieth century.

Freedom of religion was largely won by the Protestant faith and as that faith is surrendered and lost so the freedom will fade and perhaps even vanish, while those who preach it will become a beleaguered people of God. However unwelcome the notion may be, the Lord warned us of something like this and New Testament believers and many others in their wake have proved it to be so. Are such times to come again to Europe? Let all who treasure the faith once delivered to the saints work and pray for another reformation and revival which will turn nations anew to the Lord, turn back again the forces of false beliefs and irreligion and safeguard the freedoms won by our fathers in that faith at such great cost.

14.
The ongoing work

It is thirty years since EMF emerged as an independent fellowship with a British headquarters and an international field in Europe. Its roots, however, reach back another twenty-five years through the old EEC, when a basic organization was formed and when important lessons were learned which would later be incorporated in the EMF when it was established as an independent mission. Besides those lessons affecting doctrines, methods and aims of evangelistic work, there were others which influenced the internal organization at home.

Having witnessed the break-up of the EEC, which was mainly due to the lack of any body having final authority, the British Committee determined there should be only one executive body in the EMF which would have ultimate control in all its affairs at home and abroad. It was assumed that a Field Office for supervisory purposes would be needed on the Continent similar to what had previously obtained in the EEC. That arrangement was obviously needful where several branches were involved, the strongest of which was over 3,000 miles away and remote in more ways than one. It was eventually seen, however, that as Britain was a part of Europe and had a basic cultural affinity with its people, and excellent communications to boot, a separate Field Office was not really necessary.

So it is that EMF has a single Executive Committee made up of ministers, laymen and a few staff members, ministers being in the majority, two of whom serve as chairman and vice-chairman respectively. There is also a president who previously served as chairman. Advisory area councils are appointed for Ireland and Scotland and a director serves under the Executive Committee to provide day-to-day leadership of the work at home and on the field. The proximity of the field countries and the still limited extent of the work lend themselves to this simple arrangement, but substantial growth of the work in various directions could require other steps to be taken to ensure good housekeeping.

EMF has no trust funds or endowments to maintain the work; all is dependent on gifts large and small received from churches and individuals who support missionaries and projects with a faithfulness which is truly remarkable. Nothing is more striking in the entire story than the way all has been provided for, despite steady growth and raging inflation. On two or three occasions monthly allowances for missionaries have been curtailed because of financial straits; happily, the deficiencies were short-lived and all were speedily made good. We cannot detail the many instances of needs being met in amazing ways; in any case, the way they are met by regular unobtrusive gifts is no less amazing. So many of God's people have been, and still are, generous and sacrificial and the EMF is deeply indebted to them.

If a modicum of supervision and control is always required in the Lord's work, and his Word reflects this in several ways, it must not be run as a commercial enterprise based on mere financial constraints. Nor should it be an organization with that 'businesslike approach' which nowadays is confidently recommended for sure church growth with statistics, classifications, analyses, programmes and goals laid down. We serve him whose purpose and Word are for ever settled in heaven, whose going forth is from of old and whose Word and Spirit alone are our guide and enabling. This is not to suggest laxity or negligence; discipline and good order are required of missionaries, committees and home staff alike and EMF has a Confession of Faith to which all are required unreservedly to subscribe. There may have been a time when the biblical and doctrinal commitment of those involved in a fellowship like the EMF might have been taken for granted. It is no longer so; doctrinal laxity, wishful thinking, compromise and confusion have become too prevalent and it behoves us all to state clearly what we believe and to go on saying it in days of doubt and unbelief. This is why every issue of the mission's quarterly publication *Vision of Europe* carries the Confession of Faith as well as missionary reports from all parts of the field.

Missionary organizations like EMF are thought by some friends to be unbiblical because they are not specifically church-based. To treat this issue fully would require much more than a paragraph in this account. While one can respect the viewpoint of the friends who hold it, there are certainly practical considerations which make it very difficult to maintain as an inflexible rule. These include the complexities of field situations, the existence of missionaries from several groups and the general situation in the home base, Britain, where many churches are mixed and divided and the religious scene is so diverse.

The 1689 Baptist Confession, partly echoing the Westminster Confession, states that 'There are circumstances concerning the worship of God and the government of the church, common to human actions and societies, which are to be ordered in the light of nature and Christian prudence according to the general rules of the Word which are always to be observed.' If this statement cannot be regarded as finally authoritative, it goes quite a way towards countenancing missionary and other organizations which, though not narrowly resting in a church framework, are yet serving churches in a capacity which is itself thoroughly biblical.

Assuming there is a place for missionary societies, there are certain constraints within which they should invariably function, both on the home fronts and in field locations. Most important of all, they should never abrogate to themselves the role of local churches, always assuming, of course, that these churches are firmly anchored to God's Word and its doctrines.

The call and appointment of missionaries, for example, are primary matters for local churches and only after they have fulfilled their responsibilities should societies with whom the prospective missionaries expect to serve become involved. The latter should at all times deal with candidate missionaries as being sent by their own churches. Societies should also be careful to avoid activities which might clash with those of local churches and impinge upon the allegiance of their members.

While recognizing the prime significance of the foregoing, one

'Guessens', E.M.F. Headquarters in Welwyn,
Hertfordshire.

has to note that in the confused church scene of our time, acting in the light of it is not always easy and is sometimes impossible. One effective missionary serving with EMF was brought up in a church belonging to a main-line denomination which has its own well-established missionary branch serving in many countries. When this young man expressed his lack of confidence in that denominational mission because of its liberalism and indicated that he wished to apply to EMF his church refused to recommend or to support him. EMF had no alternative but to check and test the candidate's call, gifts and spirituality as best it could, in other words to do what his home church should have been doing as the instrument of the Holy Spirit. It was the Spirit who sovereignly directed that Barnabas and Saul should be separated for the mission to the Gentiles but it was physically done by the Antioch church. The church prayed and laid hands on the two missionaries, thereby identifying itself with the Spirit's will. This is still the privilege and role of a church and no society should lightly take it into its own hands.

As in the home scene, so on the field, a society must not usurp the place and functions which are rightly those of a church. Where a church has been formed it should be led and encouraged as an indigenous body of believers in biblical principles of church order and government. A society through its members may certainly help in many ways, but in doing so must ever guard against a lordly attitude towards, or sway over local believers. This may mean a young church through its own self-government occasionally making mistakes but, alas, this is the story of churches, including some with long-established order in home countries.

Recent times have seen evangelical missions coming under attacks for reasons not all that common in earlier days. One which European missions have to contend with in more than one country is based on a charge of 'colonialism', a charge which missions in Third World situations are facing in a greater degree. In Europe British and American missionaries have been castigated particularly for their emphases and for methods which are alien to historic cultures, and regrettably there is some justification for this criticism. Some missionaries are unable to adapt from what is customary in their home scene to what is culturally acceptable in the foreign scene; hence the current stress on cultural issues and the rise of training programmes in missiology. The apostle Paul dealt with the same issues and left an example which none should disregard: 'I have made myself a slave to all, that I might win the more. And to the Jews I became as a Jew, ... to those who are without law, as without law,... to the weak I became weak... for the sake of the gospel' (1 Corinthians 9:19-23, NASB).

Even so, some Christian truths are the same for all believers, of whatever nationality or culture: faith, morality, honesty and holiness are not negotiable, though some means and methods of communicating them may be adapted to take into account local outlook and practice. But there is a limit to this too; the cultures of southern Europe owe more to Catholicism than anything else, which means that truth and life which are anchored in the Bible will inevitably collide with some aspects of what prevails there. Hence the call for prudence and discretion while heeding the example set by the great apostle. The surest way of avoiding cultural clashes and thereby blunting the charges of colonialism and of paternalism is the persistent encouragement of national workers and of truly indigenous churches, both of which are grounded in biblical Christianity and able to distinguish between what is essential faith and practice and that which is amenable to local custom and culture. It may be feared that missions historically have not pursued this task as they might have done. The emphasis has been to send missionaries from the established Christian countries in large numbers, while the better and, it would seem, more scriptural way of sending high quality missionaries, whose ministry would raise up native workers, and providing adequate assistance to train these workers, has often been in default. It is indeed the more difficult way for some reasons, but surely the one with the most satisfactory results in the long term.

So far as EMF is concerned, the activities of its members in a dozen countries are almost exclusively two-fold: evangelism and church-planting. By evangelism we do not mean reaching men and women once with the gospel of Christ. We find it hard to accept that as real evangelism, though many in modern times appear to think it is. Paul, the pre-eminent New Testament evangelist, did not think so. He stayed as long as he could among those he was evangelizing to make the message plain to them, to pray for them and with them, and to gather the converts into a church fellowship with leaders appointed to care for them. One cannot think of him being satisfied with a one-off contact with a lost sinner, having a brief conversation with him and moving on to the next one. He was 'many days' among the Philippians 'announcing' the way of salvation and praying daily. Among the Thessalonians he had been like a nurse caring for her children 'because you had become dear to us'. And he reminded the Ephesian elders at Miletus how he had taught 'publicly and from house to house... repentance toward God and faith toward our Lord Jesus Christ'. He was therefore 'pure [or free] from the blood of all men'.

This surely is evangelism in its full and real sense: a persevering effort to make the truth of Christ known and understood through preaching in all its forms, continuing personal contact and prayer, the evangelist thereby becoming 'all things to all men that I may by all means save some'. If God is pleased to work exceptionally in the salvation of some sinners, using a brief contact, (one radio message, one tract, etc.), that is his sovereign prerogative and we praise him that he often does this. The responsibility of Christians is none the less plain: they are to proclaim, teach and pray wherever God places them as missionaries, pastors and church members, and to exemplify the message they preach and testify in their own lives. It is this pattern of evangelism and its goal of church-planting which EMF is committed to pursue, not as yet with the same revival blessing which James Stewart knew in pre-war eastern Europe, but in a day of small things which is not entirely without souls being saved or churches being established and built up in widely scattered parts of the barren continent.

If there is one area more than any other in which EMF has not thus far seen substantial success it is that of native churches becoming self-supporting. There is no need to labour reports of young churches that are supporting their own pastors fully or in part and others which provide financial help for widows, etc. The fact remains that all parts of western Europe have seen economic prosperity increasing in considerable measure over the second half of this century. That prosperity has not yet been comparably reflected in some of the churches established and maintained in their formative years through EMF. With wealth still extending in most countries clearer teaching and stronger leadership is now needed to bring a number of churches to the place where their own pastor and their own work in the gospel are maintained by their own finances.

It may take more time and effort to inculcate the grace of giving among people whose tradition is one of reluctantly buying grace at the behest of the Roman church. But with patience in teaching and example it will be done and EMF is committed as never before to achieving it.

In this book we have looked at modern Europe from the standpoint of Christian mission and the EMF in particular. The end result, though gratifying in some small measure, allows no complacency. Malevolent anti-Christian forces, the immensity of the field and the many complex difficulties must surely induce the question: 'Who is sufficient for these things?' Our confidence must be in God alone. It is he who gives the increase, often through revival, and our expectation and prayer are that he will do so again. Europe is so like Samaria in the days of Christ, yet revival there had large numbers testifying that 'This is indeed the Christ, the Saviour of the world.'

Samaria had false religion, a paganism which was intermingled with vestiges of Old Testament beliefs, as reflected in the words of the woman at the well: 'Our fathers worshipped in this mountain.' Even so, she and other Samaritans were expecting the Messiah. Moreover, the Jews had no dealings with the Samaritans, although once a year the Jews perversely prayed for the very people they otherwise shunned. Samaria also knew moral degeneration, for the woman was living with her sixth man, who was not her husband.

Modern Europe today is much like Samaria. What religion there is, except for small and scattered groups of evangelicals, is false, with elementary gospel truths overlaid and almost obliterated by man-made tenets. 'We worship in this mountain' could be said by vast numbers who do not know the throne of grace or what it is to worship God in spirit and in truth. Like Samaria too, missions have historically had no dealings with Europeans and perhaps few have really prayed for them either. As for its moral state, Samaria typifies Europe to an alarming degree. Yet he who brought light and life to Samaria can bring it to Europe still, and it is for this above all that we must work and pray. The key to the Samaritan blessing was that Christ himself was there: 'He must needs go through Samaria' (John 4:4). 'He abode there two days. And many more believed'

(John 4:40-41). He is blessing. He is revival, and there is none other.

An old Welsh revival hymn speaks of the Man at Jacob's well having traversed through Samaria, and says, 'Let him traverse among us now!' Let the business of churches, missions and all worthy evangelism be to take Christ to lost sinners, and may grace and power be given to do this aright, for nothing else is going to meet the need of Europe and the world.

WELWYN BIOGRAPHIES

GOD'S OUTLAW
The story of William Tyndale
Brian Edwards

When William Tyndale set out to provide the first printed New Testament in English he was forced to do so in defiance of the king, the pope and almost every person in authority. Compelled to flee his homeland, he continued with his work of translating while slipping from city to city in Germany, Holland and Belgium in an attempt to avoid his enemies. His story is one of poverty, danger and ceaseless labour to give the English-speaking people their most priceless heritage, the Scriptures in their mother tongue. The cover photograph is from the film GOD'S OUTLAW © Grenville Film Productions.

Large paperback, 174 pages.
ISBN 0 85234 161 X.

'...a stirring historical narrative, it is full of many spiritual gems which enlighten and strengthen the reader.'

Grace Magazine

THE WOLF FROM SCOTLAND
The story of Robert Reid Kalley - pioneer missionary
William B. Forsyth

This is the gripping story of Robert Reid Kalley, telling of the work of God in bringing the gospel of Jesus Christ to the Portuguese island of Madeira and to the people of Brazil. Kalley's work, largely unknown, rightly takes its place amongst the great missionary endeavours of such men as William Carey, David Livingstone and Adoniram Judson. His evident love for his hearers and his simple everyday witness in the course of his work will be a stirring challenge to the reader.

Large paperback, 240 pages,
ISBN 0 85234 256 X.

THE GOSPEL PEDLAR:
The story of John Berridge and the eighteenth-century revival
Nigel Pibworth

Counted among the friends of John Newton, George Whitefield, John Wesley, Lady Huntingdon and Henry Venn, John Berridge of Everton opens a window into the whole of the Evangelical Awakening.

This fascinating biography of the 'forgotten' preacher of Bedfordshire paints John Berridge as the unconventional pedlar of the gospel whose directness of speech earned him the reputation of being 'quaint', and 'eccentric'.

Large paperback, 320 pages,
ISBN 0 85234 236 5.

'Mr Pibworth has put us all in his debt by this well-researched and masterly biography.'

Banner of Truth

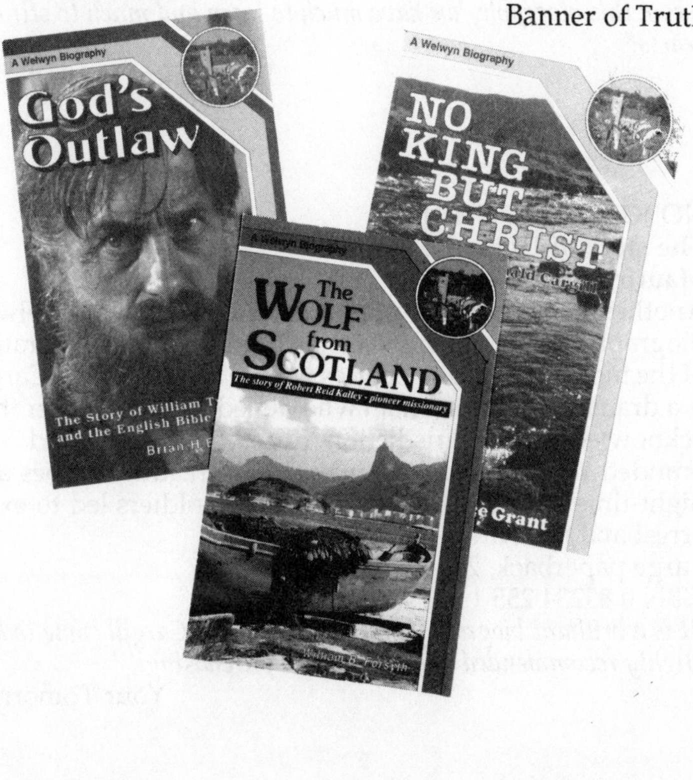

GOD SENT REVIVAL
The story of Asahel Nettleton and the Second Great Awakening
J.F. Thornbury
Following the Great Awakening under the leadership of such men as Jonathan Edwards and George Whitefield, the close of the eighteenth century in America saw a second period of revival.

One of the evangelists to emerge at this time was Asahel Nettleton, who was one of the greatest evangelists in the history of the church. Literally thousands were converted under his ministry - and spurious converts were the exception rather than the rule!

Large paperback, 240 pages, ISBN 0 85234 099 0
'Biography and history at its best.'

Fellowship

'From this biography we have much to learn and much to stir our hearts.'

Evangelical Presbyterian

NO KING BUT CHRIST
The story of Donald Cargill
Maurice Grant
Another addition to the popular and fast-growing Welwyn Biography series, set in the colourful days of the restoration of the monarchy under Charles II. The life of Donald Cargill is a dramatic story of a man who defied the king rather than acknowledge his jurisdiction over the church and was branded rebel and traitor, whose hairbreadth escapes and night-time journeys to avoid pursuing soldiers led to exile, arrest and ultimately to the gallows.

Large paperback, 272 pages,
iSBN 0 85234 255 1.
'It is a brilliant biography and one that made Cargill come to life! Highly recommended and well worth purchasing!'

Your Tomorrow

A HEART SET FREE
The life of Charles Wesley
Arnold Dallimore

Charles Wesley is well known as the 'sweet singer' of Methodism - the most gifted and most prolific of all English hymnwriters. His hymns are an exhilarating expression of the evangelical faith and mood of the revival of the eighteenth century. His gift of expressing prayer and praise in great simplicity, and faithfully recording the 'ups and downs' of the Christian life, has enriched and encouraged the whole church.

It is, however, a popular misconception that Charles was the hymnwriter and his brother John the preacher. In this new biography Arnold Dallimore firmly establishes Charles as much more than just a poet and puts him in his rightful place in Methodism's history, as one of the most powerful of the open-air field preachers of the revival and an indefatigable evangelist who spoke 'in demonstration of the Spirit and of power'.

Arnold Dallimore has written popular biographies on Spurgeon and Irving and his definitive two-volume biography on Whitefield has been widely acclaimed.

Large paperback, 272 pages,
ISBN 0 85234 249 7.

'Superbly readable and inspiring offering on the "sweet singer" of the Methodist revival... enthusiastically recommended!'

Redemption

